TRAVELS
THROUGH TIME

LEARNING ABOUT THE PAST,
TO UNDERSTAND THE PRESENT
AND CREATE OUR FUTURE

CARLOS LAYA

DEDICATION

I dedicate this book to my family and friends, who always eagerly encouraged me to continue with this fascinating project.

To all the readers, with the hope of bringing them entertainment, knowledge, and deep reflection.

To the new generations, with the aim of making a positive impact on them.

ACKNOWLEDGEMENTS

Thanks to my wife for her unwavering support; we make the best team.

To my children Carlos José and José David, for their contributions to the development of the book.

And most especially, to my dear friend Arnaldo García Perez for his valuable time and meticulous dedication in reviewing the manuscript, as well as for the excellent prologue.

FOREWORD

Man is a reflection of his being. And that being is seasoned by the blend of life experiences that shape and define us as human beings. Our personality is the sum of our feelings, values, and emotions, which make us very selective when choosing companions for our adventures. Perhaps, in this process of socialization, through trials and errors, we gradually find ourselves gravitating towards those individuals who share common feelings and make us feel comfortable in their company. This is not a simple process and it unfolds throughout our lives, so the number of guests in this particular club will be determined by the magnitude of our demands. Friendship, as they define it, is a truly genuine feeling that occurs between two individuals and is based on selflessness, service, and solidarity. To these great values and behaviors, I can personally add respect, humanity, commitment, and loyalty as some of the values that I personally treasure as measures to pass the test of true friendship. Not many pass all the subjects, and given that, the primary group becomes a small but great team.

I met Carlos Laya over 15 years ago in the city of Valencia, Venezuela. My professional activities led me to work with many companies in need of support in developing their human talent, and my social-solidarity actions led me to participate in events and activities where I could contribute in some way for the benefit of people.

Carlos was present in both scenarios. From the beginning, an undefined affinity arose between us. His involvement in the management tasks of FUNDANICA (Foundation for Children with Cancer in Carabobo State) led us to carry out some activities together in support of their organization. And then, when I was called by his company, where as Sales Manager he did a fantastic job, we collaborated in developing and training his work team. It was there that this true friendship began to develop.

Then came permanent contacts and collaborations in other common interests such as radio and the production of engaging programs. Always hand in hand with engaging in uplifting activities that would elevate and strengthen our essential values for life. That was our main connection. Fate had in store for us a physical separation, each for different reasons, as we embarked on migration to different continents and countries. This, however, instead of diminishing our contact, made it more limited but of higher quality. When Carlos Laya called me to share the news that he was about to embark on a literary adventure and start writing his first novel, I felt great joy in this event. First, it confirmed to me that Carlos was unwavering in his purpose of adding value to the lives of others. And secondly, because in a way, with the news, he made me a partaker in his project.

An incredible and fruitful adventure began for both of us. His enthusiasm and joy in sharing that dream translated into a novel led him to invest hours in continuous production of material, and we started an enriching exchange of impressions and ideas that led him to that great final product he presents today. His first great literary work.

Today, I have the honor of presenting to you his first novel, "Travels Through Time," a work of fiction that encapsulates all the potential and talent my friend has cultivated over the years. I feel excited and privileged to be the bearer of this seed of imagination that is about to sprout in your hands.

Within these pages, you will find the roots of a story that will take us through winding paths and immerse us in an unknown universe. As we progress through the reading, we will experience the evolution of vibrant characters and encounter unexpected situations that will challenge us to reflect on our own existence. At the heart of this novel, we will find a courageous and dreamy protagonist named Glem, whose thirst for adventure will lead him to explore worlds beyond the tangible. Through his eyes, we will discover a universe where fantasy intertwines with reality, where boundaries blur, and where dreams are defined as the fuel that drives our lives. I must confess that, while reading Glem's adventures, I cannot help but imagine a young, intelligent, and spirited Carlos Laya, giving his best in every endeavor he undertakes, whether it is in the family, academic, or social sphere.

With "Travels Through Time" we will embark on a journey that is more than just interesting, opening ourselves to different visions and experiences. The challenge of Glem's adventure will bring us closer to exploring uncharted aspects of the characters involved in his adventures. As one of the fundamental elements of the novel, they help us reinforce essential life values. Each journey will serve as a frame of reference for a significant value, and from there, numerous learning about life, the characters involved, and, most importantly, an opportunity for reflection for us.

This prologue is an invitation to a unique and extraordinary journey. As the words come to life, we will encounter characters that will challenge us, make us laugh, and deeply move us. We will traverse marvelous places, confront both the past and the future, and immerse ourselves in ethical dilemmas that will make us reflect on our own humanity.

My friend Carlos, as a budding writer, has poured his soul into every page of this book. This prologue is my way of applauding his courage, encouraging him to continue on this thrilling literary journey, and reaffirming my friendship and support. I am confident that those who embark on this story will be rewarded with intense emotions and astonishing discoveries.

So, without further ado, welcome to "Travels Through Time" ...

Arnaldo García Pérez

CHAPTER I

THE INTERVIEW

"Love knows no grudges and does not require apologies, it is only patient and feeds on itself, because all that exists is love"

Glem was getting ready to head to the library, a place he had frequented before, but this trip would be very different from those in the past. He wore a dark grey tailcoat, the same-color linen pants, a mother-ironed pristine white shirt, and a yellow tie. Even though it was his first job interview, he was incredibly confident. He made the decision to take public transportation that day instead of his usual bicycle because he was unsure of the travel hours and wanted to prevent any delays.

He arrived thirty minutes prior to his appointment at the Ottawa Parliament Building complex. He then went to the front door and displayed the document attesting to his meeting at the parliament library. After being granted admission, he made his way to the complex's north side. He soon discovered himself in a stunning Victorian-era corridor that connected the library and the parliament. Outside, he could see the neo-gothic style galleries, fire doors, sandstone block walls, buttress arches, arched windows, towers, and delicate pinnacles that graced the stunning circular structure. Regarding the interior, were admired the lovely pine galleries decorated with floral designs, coats of arms, masks, and mythical creatures. The wide reading room was well framed by its exquisite dome-shaped ceiling. In the middle of the chamber was a white marble statue of a young Queen Victoria, while marble busts of the prince and princess of Wales (Albert Edward and Alexandra of Denmark), Sir John Sandfield Macdonald, and Sir Étienne Taché Pascual were also present.

While waiting for the interview, Glem observed an old friend was approaching the inner door of the library. It was Mya, a pleasant Indigenous descent woman in her late sixties who worked in the maintenance area and was also a wonderful conversationalist. As usual, they started a fun conversation that inevitably led to Glem's favourite subject: discovering the elements of indigenous culture that have persisted to this day as well as some native terms.

When it was time for the interview, the front door unlocked. Mrs. Trembley, the oldest employee there, was standing on the opposite side with a charming young man named Marcos —who is of Latin American heritage— and Sandra Rizzi, a stunning and thin young redhead with freckles and green eyes. Despite being best friends throughout high school, the girl's expression of astonishment when she first saw Glem dressed stylishly was obvious. And there he was, a tall and attractive young man of 20 years with a stocky frame, straight black hair, a fair complexion, and slanted eyes that indicated his Filipino background and 6 feet, 2.8 in tall. Everyone in the room was a good friend of the youngster because he frequently spent hours there reading, one of his hobbies. Mrs. Trembley informs him as he reaches the information desk area:

—Glem, I appreciate your punctuality and I beg you to be patient while we wait for the other candidate, who has already notified us that he will be five minutes late.

In response, the boy made a kind motion to show that everything was alright before going to meet his two pals. When they first saw him, they teased him, saying they hardly recognized him because he was not only incredibly elegant but also wearing outfits that were perfectly appropriate for the situation. The young guy's appearance that day was significantly different from how he typically appeared, as he usually traveled on his trusty bicycle while dressed in sportswear and toting a rucksack filled with everything he required. While they were having a funny talk in the hallway of one of the exquisite pine wood galleries, Mrs. Trembley's voice interrupted them.

—Our other participant is already present; could you, Glem, please get closer so we may begin the interview.

The boy could not believe his eyes when he saw his competitor as he approached the counter. A young man with a slim build, a European manner, and beautifully dressed in a suit was standing next to the interviewer. Despite being unable to include him in his circle of friends, Glem knew him well. He was the older brother of Sandra. Glem, who is now a bit perplexed, turns to see where her best friend is, while he wonders why she would have pushed me so hard to apply for this post if she knew that the other most probable applicant would be her arrogant brother, who is also a law school debate champion. She made a sign that they both recognized when they caught a glimpse of him. She made multiple touches to her temple with her index finger to signify <<remain focused >>.

As soon as the interview began, the moderator spoke first.

—Mr. Glem, I'd like to introduce you to Mr. Enzo Rizzi, and please welcome Mr. Glem Suárez —the septuagenarian spoke as she gestured for a handshake to be exchanged between them—. Among a group of about five hundred applications, you were chosen for the final interview based on your profile and the essay that each applicant provided.

The young university student then interrupted the woman before she could finish her intervention, saying.

—I'm sorry for the delay, but I had to stop and speak for a little while with a good friend who is a member of the parliament. He knew about my interview and wanted to use the occasion to provide me some insightful advice —the young student spoke in an arrogant manner—. And I also want to let you know that I currently have a minor otitis problem, therefore I need to use this hearing aid you can see here —pointing to his right ear, the eloquent young guy concluded.

When Enzo interrupted the interview, Mrs. Trembley appeared a little uneasy. She then went on.

—Okay, let's move on with the interview, and I kindly ask that you refrain from making any further disruptions because the public's access time is soon to begin —in a serious voice, the librarian spoke—. Each applicant will be given the opportunity to respond to three questions, two of which will be about the library, which I will ask. The last one, which must be connected to a subject related to parliament, will be sent by each of you to the other. We shall begin with Mr. Glem Suárez —and directing his gaze towards the youngster, she prepared to ask him—. Could you please let us know when the library first opened?

History was one of the young man's favorite reading genres, and he was particularly knowledgeable about the republican history of Canada's legislative library. So, without further ado, he started to respond.

.

—After 17 years of building, this enclosure opened its doors in 1876. Most of its books came from Upper and Lower Canada's parliamentary libraries towards the end of the 18th century as well as Queen Victoria's personal library —the young guy precisely explained.

The librarian complimented that quick and precise response before turning to the law student.

—When did the first fire in the parliament occur, Mr. Enzo Rizzi, and how was the library saved?

That young man started speaking as though making a plea in front of a court.

.

—Before I begin, I'd like to greet everyone in attendance and thank them for this interview, which

I had been eagerly anticipating —the future lawyer spoke while adjusting the little device he was wearing in his ear repeatedly, as if it were a highly strung tic—. Now, to answer your question, that regrettable incident took place in 1916 when, for unknown reasons, a low-intensity fire began in the complex's central building and quickly grew out of control. Fortunately, the library was spared damage thanks to the prompt action of one of its employees, who ordered the iron doors to be closed, separating this space from the rest of the building, and thanks to the city's firemen' quick action —the young man explained, pausing between each of his ideas as if he were giving a speech before a jury.

The meeting's facilitator commended the university student for making a pertinent point during his intervention. She urged him to be more succinct and flowing in his responses, though, at the same time. The young man speaks up in response to this request, saying.

—I apologise if my behaviour causes any discomfort; if so, I state that I do it unintentionally. In my defence, I wish to say that my status as a law student at the esteemed University of Ottawa, my aptitude for debate, and my desire to one day become an outstanding parliamentarian, cause me to develop in this way.

After that intervention, the librarian realised that instead of waiting for Enzo to comply with her rules, she should move forward with the interview while embracing his unusual behaviour to finish it as quickly as possible. In this way, she picked up the conversation and turned to Glem to address him.

—Mr. Suárez, could you please tell us who Albert Edward was? —the woman spoke while indicating one of the reading room's busts.

The young man then responded without any hesitation.

—This person was the Prince of Wales before taking the throne from his mother, Queen Victoria, at the start of the 20th century. He modernised the British army and is renowned for fostering friendly relations between his nation and other European nations, getting him the moniker "The Pacifier."

The cultured hostess expressed her satisfaction with the adolescent's straightforward response once more by nodding her head, and she immediately asked her final query.

—Could Mr. Rizzi give us a brief overview to Sir John Sanfield Macdonald? —the woman asked, indicating with her thumb and index finger that she was anticipating a brief response.

Enzo then assumes an upright stance as if he were going to give a speech as he gets ready to respond to the inquiry.

—Born in Canada, Sir. John Sanfield Macdonald was hmm... a renowned attorney and royal advisor who hmm... held the position of prime minister of the then-unified Province of Canada for two years —the future lawyer spoke with considerable difficulty and frequently used fillers, as if he had trouble coming up with the right words; this seemed unlikely for a speaker of his stature, but he yet continued with his presentation—. He was also Ontario's first Prime Minister hmm... and the first person to hold that post in this province. —thus, he concluded his speech while displaying some nervousness, much to the surprise of those in attendance.

After that strange speech, Mrs. Trembley approaches the stage and invites Enzo to ask a question to Glem. The young Rizzi then quickly changed his attitude and addressed his interlocutor with a glance that emanated a halo of malice.

—Glem, please I'd like to congratulate you because you appear to be a parliament employee; I'm just wondering if you purchased the attire from a souvenir shop in Ottawa —Enzo concluded in a sarcastic voice.

Glem answered with calm and cleverness.

—No, Enzo; I chose these outfits because I am so confident that I would get hired that I would be happy to begin working today if they asked me to.

Following that surprise response, Enzo rushes to speak as the two young employees and even the typically very formal librarian are grinning covertly. He then asks the following inquiry while grinning mischievously once again.

—Please list three exemplary qualities about our former first minister Arthur Smith, Mr. Glem.

Glem's normally jovial face changed into a calm, even slightly obfuscated, expression at that same moment. Up until that point, the youngster had felt ready to respond to any inquiry, but he could not deny that this one had misplaced him. After doing a thorough investigation, his adversary had carefully selected that query after identifying the cheery boy's weakness. Mrs. Trembley and Marcos were looking forward to Glem's answer to the simple question, and their confidence grew as they knew they were talking about his paternal grandfather. Only Sandra, however, was aware that her best friend would not respond to that inquiry even if it cost him the job. The two friends then came face to face, and the guy gave her a look as if he were questioning why she had betrayed him. She responded with signs that she had no idea how it could have happened. When Glem spoke to respond, the tense moment came to an end.

—I am fully aware of the potential consequences of my answer, but I still will act. I'd rather not comment on the leadership of the former Prime Minister Smith in this instance.

Some people in attendance found that remark oddly shocking, however Enzo couldn't help but smile triumphantly, as if a mischievous youngster had just gotten away with something. The older woman then motions with her hand to Mr. Suárez, inviting him to ask his opponent the question now. At that moment, the haughty university student approaches Glem and pats him on the shoulder as if to reassure him that everything is fine. However, he continues to display a cocky attitude while standing close to him, which Glem found suspicious given the other odd behaviours Enzo exhibited during the meeting. So, when the lad thought about the last question, a brilliant thought came to him, and he swiftly prepared to speak.

—Mr. Enzo Rizzi, could you please tell us who Mya Oneida is?

The three spectators' shocked expressions eventually gave way to knowing laughs. While the anxious Enzo walked erratically, he kept stroking the tiny device in his ear and kept saying the unknown name repeatedly as if he were waiting for an answer to arrive from somewhere other than his thoughts. He gave up after a while and asked Glem to identify the person who everyone else in the room knew about but him. His opponent spoke up and responded to him.

—The second-oldest employee of this library after Mrs. Trembley is the highly respected Mya Oneida, a lovely woman —when she heard her name, the sweet lady who was finishing up the reading room's cleaning looked up from what she was doing. She bends to the distance in front of Enzo's astonished face as if to express her greeting; at that very moment, Glem proceeded with his dissertation—. I believe she is more Canadian than any of the others here since she is a direct descendent of the Cree people who lived in the north. She is given special significance simply by she is regarded as a valuable individual by everyone who works in this illustrious setting.

The irascible Enzo responded right away. He yanked off that tiny device, which more closely resembled a wireless hearing aid than a sound amplifier, in a furious manner, and addressed the audience in a rebellious manner.

—I think that what just transpired was in poor taste since how I was expected to be able to respond to that question, and Mrs. Trembley made it very plain that we should discuss figures associated with the Canadian Parliament —that young man responded angrily.

His opponent responded without hesitation.

—Your response, Rizzi, is extremely odd to me since, being the competent litigator that you are, you are well aware that most cases are won before to the presentations, and that this always depends on your preparation and the volume of pertinent data you have gathered. —Glem spoke once more, speaking this time with the same confidence—. I believe that to be considered for this fantastic organisation, we should get to know it better, learn to know it inside and out, and even be willing to work for it freely when the need arises   —that smart young man culminated as if it were the end of a debate.

When Enzo felt exposed to such tremendous exposure, he desperately tried to make a point in the hopes of standing out as something that would be advantageous to him.

—Mrs. Trembley, I believe you should also consider the candidates' proficiency in other relevant areas, such as the number of languages they speak. In my case, as I noted in my resume, I speak fluent English, French, and Italian, and this would be very helpful during the guided tours given to visitors to the location —the young Rizzi ended his speech with another instance of his arrogant attitude.

Glem, for his part, responded right away.

—It is an amazing observation, Enzo, and I must thank you because you have suddenly emerged as my best advocate for the post given, that I am fluent in English, French, Spanish, and Filipino —he speaks calmly.

Enzo's expression of annoyance was clear prior to that intervention. Mrs. Trembley glances at her watch and realises that the library is about to open to the public in a few minutes, so she addresses the two young people right away.

—Thanks, gentlemen we appreciate your time, and we will now end the interview. Please check your emails for the interview's conclusion. I hope you have the most wonderful day —said that formal lady as she led both to the room's entrance.

Enzo stepped more quickly to exit the building through the main door as soon as they had both left that room. When he got there, he paused, pulled out his phone, and pretended to be conversing while making sure Glem left the area. Then, he proceeded to the lovely park on the hill where his best friend John was. Sandra had asked Mrs. Trembley for a short leave of absence at this time, and when she arrived at the door leading to the park, she saw her brother and his buddy engaged in an argument; John was using a laptop, and from what she could see, he was trying to excuse himself. She immediately realised that her brother had outside assistance during the interview.

Glem went to see his mom in the interim. He thought he had some things to say to her.

When he arrived at the "La Sagrada Familia" church, she was there, always with kids and teenagers, doing what she loved most: teaching.

Ada Suárez was a beautiful woman; despite being 46 years old, her stylized figure and height of five feet and five inches made her appear much younger. In addition, her Asian features, tan skin colour, and straight black hair that reached her waist made her very attractive.

Her eyes lit up when she saw her son. She then extended an invitation to him to come to the small church hall where she regularly taught language sessions to the neighborhood's kids and teenagers. Mother and youngster hugged after class and struck up a friendly conversation.

—What do I owe you for this fantastic visit, son? Why can't you wait till dinner? What do you want to tell me? —Ada said, trusting her infallible mother's intuition.

—You know me as well as if you were my mother —they both started giggling when Glem responded, and he continued—. I just finished a job interview, and I want to share with you my immediate plans.

—Okay, let's have some tea then —after 700 feet of walking, they came to a location known as "The Green Door."

It was a charming eatery with simple design and an interesting selection of organic vegetarian food, along with delicious pastries, which made it the preferred gathering spot for Ada and everyone else that frequented that neighbourhood. It was summer in Ottawa, and the weather was perfect as they sat at a table outside the establishment, ordered two teas, and enjoyed a delicious cake.

—What updates do you have for me, son? —asked the mother, curious as to why they had such a lovely and unexpected meeting.

—I wanted to let you know that I have made the decision to give up my pastime of hiking and spend more time at home. I even followed Sandra's advice, and I just went to a job interview to join the staff of the Parliament Library —the guy commented, clearly excited.

—Son, I confess that I am conflicted —the mother said in a tone that was both worried and thoughtful—. There is nothing that makes me happier than having you at home, but on the other hand, I know that you are a free soul, just like your father was, and I would not want you to give up one of your greatest passions for anyone, and that includes me. You know very well that one day your father gave up the life that fulfilled him to be with us, and that resulted in his passing away, and I tell you something, I could not bear the loss of the two men I have loved the most in my life for similar reasons —the mother concluded with tears in her eyes.

—I completely understand your viewpoint, mother, and trust me when I say that this decision is primarily about me and what I want to accomplish with my life moving forward —that young man spoke with the maturity that defined him—. Although I spent the past year exploring the most important trails in Canada, partly as a way to cope with my father's passing by being in nature, I now feel that it is time to start moving in a new direction and projecting what I want for the future. Although I have thoroughly enjoyed every moment of reflection, every new landscape I have discovered, and every person I have met on so many paths, I am still very young and know that I must find a balance. Additionally, the mind is powerful, and reading may also inspire intense and lovely trips via the imagination.

Thanks to his thoughtful response, the mother felt more at ease at that moment. After that, they both decided to talk about the boy's adventures and trips, having a blast in the process.

When Glem returned after his morning run and other workout the following day, he checked his mail and discovered Mrs. Trembley's response. A pleasant and professional message advising him that he had been hired for the position and was expected to start on Monday was sent to him. His phone rang five minutes later —it was Sandra—, she gave him a call to congratulate him on his new position. She wanted to celebrate the accomplishment by inviting him to supper at the customary Italian restaurant because it was Friday. Glem thanked her for the invitation and perplexed, enquired as to how she was aware of the outcome. She informed him those just moments earlier, she had overheard her brother speaking with the librarian.

Sandra revealed over the phone that Enzo made up his mind to visit the library after learning via email that he had not been chosen. When he arrived, he informed Mrs. Trembley that he was perplexed as to why he had not been selected despite having the support of a key lawmaker. The always correct lady responded that while the organisation she works for values any government figure's suggestions, she has full authority when it comes to matters involving the library employees. She yet dared to remind him that Mr. Glem Suárez also had the endorsement of a key official in the government to make that point even more clear. Lena Smith, his aunt and the current Minister of Canadian Culture and Heritage, When presented with that reasoning, the haughty university student was forced to politely thank her for his time and bid her farewell, because he was well aware that his contact in parliament could not possibly compete with that woman's successful political career.

In contrast to what he expected, Glem was disappointed when he learned that his aunt had played a role in the choice because he did not know which aspect might have been more important: his qualifications and performance during the interview, or that significant recommendation.

The fact is this feeling of disappointment was mainly due to his personal decision to cut ties with his paternal family. Faced with this dilemma, and to dispel his doubts, he decided to break his pride and call his aunt.

He called the minister's number, and as usual, his assistant answered. The secretary's professional, almost robotic answer changed to a warm, sincere greeting as soon as the young guy introduced himself. She requested that he wait while she found her boss. After a brief delay, Lena picked up the phone and spoke to her nephew while clearly excited.

—My darling Glem, how wonderful to hear from you. You have no idea how much your call moves me. Please let me know how you and your mother are doing.

—We are all very well, Aunt Lena, thanks for asking —the youngster answered in a cold manner—. I am aware that as a result of my choice, we have not spoken for a while, but I am phoning you now to ask how much of an impact you had on the selection to work as an assistant in the legislative library's reading room.

—Dear nephew I won't deny that I was aware of your application because my good friend Mrs. Trembley was kind enough to let me know. After I asked her to list me as a reference on your application, she expressed her appreciation for my offer and let me know that she thought you were the best candidate for the position because of how well she knows you and the close relationships you have had with everyone who works there —his aunt spoke as though she were confessing.

—In that case, I want to thank you and let you know that after hearing everything you said, I feel more at ease —the guy responded in the same icy manner. But before he could depart, his aunt stepped into speaks to continue their conversation.

—Glem, I might understand why you have decided to get away from us —she begins by using a friendly voice—. But I want you to keep in mind that I really loved my brother, and that love extended to you and your mother as well. Like everyone else, I regret his passing. However, you must understand that if you harbor any grudges against your grandfather, I want you to know that I and the rest of the family do not view we as deserving of the same treatment as he did. Moreover, I want you to know that I will look out for you and your mother as long as I live because you are still my relatives and I incalculably value the love and happiness you both brought into my brother's life. I admit that your absence deeply affects me, and because I selected a challenging job in politics while living in my father's tight shadow, has caused me to reach this age without having the joy of starting a family; you are like a son to me, just like I frequently told my brother; I've been wanting to tell you all of this for a long time, and I regret not telling you sooner.

The woman's voice broke, and the boy's face drew an expression of introspection as he felt compelled to submit to a truth the size of a mountain that had just come into view. He responded this time in a cordial manner, as if pleading for forgiveness.

—Kind aunt, your words have impacted me deeply; I apologize for my behavior and thank you for your patience and wisdom. From this point forward, we will be the same again, perhaps even better, and I know that we will be more united, just as my father would have wanted. Once again, I apologize for the ways I've behaved.

—Son of my heart, you must know that love holds no grudges and requires no apologies; it is only patient and feeds on itself, because all that exists is love. Any other aspect that we feel different is just our distracted mind; the key is to return to the source, which is love.

The conversation ended, and that boy felt great peace and thought, «it's time to reconnect with my family».

THE PAST

When night fell, Glem prepared to join Sandra in the celebration. Once more, he decided to skip her usual athletic attire in favor of a dress that fell between casual and classy. Something in that wandering, carefree young man was shifting.

He took a taxi to "La Roma". A classy eatery situated in Little Italy. With a subtle black and white design, a fine menu with Italian titles for the dishes, and a dinner that can satisfy the pickiest diners.

When he got there, he saw that his companion was already there and talking to Ms. Maria, the establishment's owner and a close friend to both of them, in Italian. The girl greeted him enthusiastically when he approached the table, and the youngster reciprocated using the few Italian words his friend had given him. Following their welcomes, the lovely lady left them and went about her business in the crowded area. Glem observed his companion staring at him when he sat down, as if trying to figure out the changes he had been exhibiting since his return from his most recent hiking excursion. Glem exhibited a look of intense curiosity on his end, as if he was entitled to an explanation for all the questions going through his mind. She told him before he could speak since she was quite familiar with him.

—Please allow me to clarify —she began as if pleading for patience from her listener—. I was aware that my brother was also applying for the job, but he decided to do so after I persuaded you to do so. If I did not tell you, it was because I believed it would be wise to get the current result. Let's say you're asking why I'd rather have you at the library than my brother. In such scenario, it's simple; he wasn't interested in the position and only wanted to be near to lawmakers for his own gain. In addition, it's possible that he will frequently find an excuse to miss his schedule and will ask me to fill in for him.

Regarding how he discovered that talking about your grandfather was your weakness, I freely admit that it was my responsibility. One day, his equally skilled girlfriend asked me about you and said that, despite not knowing you well, she could not understand how someone could be so happy all the time. She added that she would kill to know if there was a way to break you away from that state. At the time, I fell for her deception because I believed her words to be sincere. I only ventured to confide in her that the few times I had accidentally struck up a talk about your grandfather and seen you acting a little out of place. I really apologize as I have just realized everything was a trap —Sandra concluded, giving a remorseful shrug of her shoulders.

—Nothing should be apologized for —he gave her a wide smile as he responded—. We are best friends, and I am confident that we couldn't hurt one another.

—I appreciate you being so understanding —the young lady responded with a sense of relief, but her expression changed to one of doubt at that point—. Now that you bring it up, I completely agree with you. Because of our close friendship, you know a lot about me, but I don't know anything about your paternal family. If you could fill me in on this, I'd even venture to say it would be therapeutic for you.

—Perhaps you're right, —said the young man thoughtfully—. But I warn you; it's a long story.

—Those are the ones I like the most —the girl replied, settling into her chair as though trying to be as comfortable as she could—. We have the entire night, so you can speak without leaving out any details; I've always liked the passion with which you tell stories —she concluded, drawing a smile to her lips.

When the waiter arrived, he inquired as to if they were prepared to place an order. Before placing her order, Sandra, who had previously discussed the menu with the kind Mrs. Maria, suggested the dish that her companion had noticed on their previous visit as one of the few foods he hadn't tasted. He nodded his agreement with the suggestion. When the waiter asked what they wanted to drink, she ordered a bottle of Rubio Toscana. An exquisite Italian red wine with a fresh aroma of red cherries, violets, and black currants, subtle notes of spices, good structure and balance, and pleasant aromatic persistence. Glem spoke to his friend, pleased by the outstanding decision.

—I would have rented a tailcoat if I had known the level of celebration. —he said with a sarcastic grin.

—The reality is that beating my arrogant brother at an interview is unusual for someone who is not yet enrolled in college, and what's more impressive is that I found out he had assistance —In response, she expressed some shame at his brother's behaviour; in the meantime, the youngster made a gesture like when you're just putting a puzzle together in your head, she then continued—. Also, this dinner will be fun because throughout the course of our five years of friendship, you have learned everything there is to know about my family, and now it is my turn to learn more about yours.

Glem, who had always been very reserved on the matter, recognised his friend's right to hear his narrative and agreed with her that this situation would provide catharsis. Glem urged the waiter not to interrupt them, saying that they would let him know if they needed anything as soon as they delivered the bottle of wine and served the food. That guy began to recount his story after he sighed deeply, as though getting ready to make a voluntary confession.

—I'll begin my story with describing the history of my maternal family in the Philippines to set the scene —that young man started with the eloquence that was characteristic of him when he told stories—. My grandparents came from privileged backgrounds. My grandfather was an outspoken opponent of the US colonisation of the island in the 1930s and served as editor of a famous newspaper in Manila, the nation's capital. South of the capital, in the lovely port city of Rosario, my grandma was a well-known educator.

My mother, the youngest of seven children, was the only one to dedicate her life to teaching, much like my grandmother. The Philippines had been self-governing for more than three decades when my mother was 25 years old. She was employed as a language instructor at the state university of Cavite at that time; Cavite is the name of the province that includes her hometown of Rosario.

She volunteered on the weekends at her family's business, a small but lovely restaurant that my grandparents had started to keep them busy in their latter years. It became well known around the region due to its waterfront position, great food, and attentive service from my family.

When a Canadian-flagged ship docked there one day, some crew members inquired about the location of the best beachside dining establishment.

The locals responded without doubt that "Las Salinas" restaurant was the best.

In an instant, the place was filled with sailors, who ate and drank as if they had gone weeks without eating. Soon, as expected, some had too many drinks. Two sailors who shared a small table near the premises door when they saw my mother pass by, —who until now has always stood out for her natural beauty—, they were extremely animated and one of them speaking in French said, *"I would like to take her to the ship and not leave the cabin for the rest of the trip"*. My mother walked back to the table and politely requested that they leave the table if they were finished eating. Since then, she had perfected five languages. She warned them that they would not tolerate vulgar comments because this was a family-run establishment. The two men were so drunk that they laughed instead of feeling uncomfortable, and this time the second man said to the first in Portuguese, *"You can see she has a bad temper; if you take her, I'll accompany you in the cabin to make sure don't let anything happen to you."* At that moment my mom exploded and yelled the same phrase at them in English, French, Portuguese and Spanish *"I want you to leave the restaurant right now, or I'll call the police,"* she only reserved the Tagalog because she knew that they would not understand the Filipino, plus she didn't want to upset his brothers. Everyone in the room turned to see the scene of the fight at that time. Before my uncles and other family members arrived at that table, a tall man who had been sitting there all along and had been absorbed in writing down accounting data in a large book suddenly stood up. Before they arrived, he had already grabbed each of the men by the arms and pushed them away from the restaurant. However, the issue was resolved, and the other men acted properly.

When they were about to close the restaurant for the evening, someone knocked on the door. When my mother said that they were no longer working, she was able to identify the person with whom she had previously assisted in resolving the unpleasant situation. My father was an attractive man. He was blond, had a stocky build, dark skin that had been browned by the sea, light eyes, was six feet and three inches tall, and had an alluring aura about him. She told me that when she saw him, she had a weird feeling. She seemed to already know him. At that very moment, without saying a word, their gazes connected and went into a trance, as if the universe had stopped —the moment Glem noticed how much his partner was engrossed in the story, he set aside what was left of his food and continued passionately. Sandra, who had already finished her plate, had her bright emerald eyes wide open and had placed her two hands holding her head as when a girl is ecstatic listening to a story—. When my mother back to his senses, she could only manage to remark that they had already closed. My father then responded by saying that he had returned for his notebook. At that same time, she recalled finding it on the table from which he got up. She therefore requested him to wait while she brings this one back.

It only took a moment, and she was utterly shocked to find that man waiting for her holding a stunning bunch of white tulips. How could this stranger possibly know the flowers she preferred?

She couldn't believe it. She handed him the book while trying to act normal and hide her surprise from her. She then hurriedly tried to enter the premises. She was outmatched by my father's skill, so he quickly moved to stand between her and the entrance. He quickly requested that she accept the bouquet as a sign of his heartfelt regret for what had occurred with his friends. He also wanted her to know that he wanted her to go with him to see that beautiful city if she didn't have any other commitments. My mother, who has always been a very self-assured woman, felt goosebumps and blush on her face, but she just took the bouquet and swerved around the man, saying «Thank you» before heading back to the local.

As soon as the daily labour of cleaning and organising the restaurant was finished, all my family members and staff departed simultaneously, and there, only ten metres from that door, was my father, standing with his hands behind his back as though in the resting position of naval officers. My mom's older brother yelled at the man and asked him what was wrong with his family when he realised it was one of the Canadian ship's crew members. My mother grabbed her brother by the arm and urged him to maintain his composure. That man had been waiting for her because they had both agreed to speak when the restaurant closed. My father remained unperturbed.

Once they were alone, she asked him what he was doing standing there. He replied that although he did not understand women very much, but one thing was clear to him: when they did not want something, they answered with a resounding «no» and that another different answers, including silence was a hidden «yes». When my mother smiled for the first time at that point, my father claimed he felt mesmerised by the beauty of her face.

She then extended an invitation to him to accompany her on a stroll along the coast as they conversed. Eventually, they arrived at a secret site concealed from view where they could hear the waves of the sea and admire the lovely full moon that night. My mother did not want to be seen travelling around the city with a stranger even if she did not have anyone in her life at that time. She therefore made the decision to show him her private refuge, where she frequently went to read, study, or take a brief break from the outside world.

She told me that she was very shocked by that man's personality because he never attempted to seduce her, didn't want to talk exclusively about himself, and wasn't even interested in learning about the specifics of her life. He dedicated himself to contemplating about and loving the places they visited, living each moment to the fullest, and engaging in stimulating conversation on literature, history, philosophies, and even astronomy. She had always thought of men of the sea as a simple folk, and she had never expected to be so impressed by their actions and thoughts. Additionally, she experienced an almost blind faith for that stranger due to an inexplicable factor.

Then, during a heated discussion over what each person's definition of life's purpose was, morning broke, and a drizzle started. There was not enough time to safely leave this location without risking getting wet. They then made the decision to seek refuge under some shrubs, which could only be sheltered essentially lying down due to their short height.

Without saying a word to her, my father quickly enfolded her in his arms to keep her warm and shield her from the few drops that filtered through the foliage. My mother returned to experience the trance in which she was unable to distinguish between time and place after being enticed by that gesture and by the lovely scent of that alluring man. She started kissing him out of instinct at that point.

My mother, who had a strict upbringing, says that it is not explained what happened at that moment. It appears a stronger force had possessed her. I was the outcome of that night —Glem appeared uncomfortable at the time for having revealed such a private matter about his mother. Sandra understood that gesture and took his hands. By staring into his eyes, she assured him that nothing was wrong and that he could trust her—. Before saying goodbye, my father escorted her to a few streets near her house at daybreak. He then took off his sailor ring and gave it to her, telling her that she was the woman he had once dreamed of and that this present was a sign that he would return for her. Although he was unable to give a precise time, his promise was as reliable as the sun's daily rise. Looking into his eyes after receiving that present and realising that his comments were true, my mother was convinced. They had a last kiss, and at that moment, she, with a malicious smile, told him, *"Nice to meet you; my name is Ada Suárez."* My father, a little embarrassed by the slip of not even having introduced himself properly, he only managed to answer, *"It has been the most wonderful evening of my life, all yours Glem Smith."*

She immediately turned around and headed back to her house while wearing an enormous smile that did not fit her face and having butterflies in her stomach as if he were her first love. For his part, my father was relieved to have located the treasure he had been searching for a long time as he headed back to his boat. The time to set sail had already passed four hours earlier, so he had to deal with the captain's haughty complain for the first time in his immaculate career as a merchant seaman once he was on board.

My father performed the function of the administration of the entire ship and was the captain's right hand. Once they sailed, my father went to his office, and there was the always detailed Peter Hole, his assistant and best friend. My father was curiously happy despite the recent meeting with the captain; in addition, Peter noticed he was holding the account book that he had forgotten in that restaurant and did not have his sailor's ring. So, with a mischievous tone, he told him that the crew's hours of concern for his absence were a total waste of time. The sudden reaction of seriousness on my father's face made his friend understand that night had meant something more than a simple rendezvous.

My father was adamant on seeing my mother again, but he first needed to organise a few things and then wait for another trip to Asia. Even though he was able to quickly organise many things, the long-awaited trip to Southeast Asia ultimately never materialised, and in fact, he saw it as being farther away due to the naval company's unforeseen decision to divert the ship's course from Asia to Central and South America.

My mother, on the other hand, was left to deal with my grandfather's strong personality alone; he believed that being pregnant was a stain on his surname, which caused her considerable grief; when his father passed away —soon after—, without his attitude toward her, it would change.

My parents used to write letters to one other back then. In each message, my father stated that he was looking for a way to return and meet with her. My mother, without going into further detail, just replied that everything was good and that she was looking forward to his return. That she kept their child a secret from him was the most amazing thing, though. She didn't want to push him to return so if he does it on his own, it was because he wanted it to be that way.

When I was four years old, my father gave up on delaying that reunion and used all his vacation time to start his journey to the Philippines. He investigated and found a merchant ship departing shortly from the crowded US port of Seattle, barely a three-hour drive from his home in Vancouver, because he was terrified of flying.

Due to a fortunate coincidence, my father's surprise journey to Las Salinas took place on a Friday, ensuring that he would find my mother working at the restaurant. The location was crowded when he arrived at six in the afternoon, so he entered and carried his bag and a huge bouquet of white tulips and stood next to the door. My uncle, the same one who had confronted him in the street years earlier, approached my mother, who extremely busy, and motioned for her to look toward the door before she realised, he was there. She immediately stopped what she was doing when she saw him and ran to give him a warm welcome. He took the flowers, inhaled deeply as he smelled them, and then set them on a small table by the door before giving her a long, passionate hug.

I got there at that same time while they were still hugging. I started working in the family business at the age of four, delivering napkins, cutlery, and spice jars to the tables. I grabbed my mother's skirt at that point, oblivious to what was happening, and informed her that a table was requesting water. My father first noticed me when they split up. He says that he immediately felt the call of the blood. He looked at my mother with an expression of bewilderment, and she only nodded while holding me in her arms. When she said, "*Glem, he is your father*" at that precise time, my first thought was, "*The sailor?*" My father carried me for the first time that day, and as he stretches out his arms to hug me, he fully detailed me in front of him. He repeatedly held me after that, and I saw how he moved as if he were describing a joyful dance. I remember feeling both odd and at ease at the same moment. My father's strength and height provided me an unfathomable sense of security.

Now you know why I don't have a Smith last name —Sandra nodded her head in agreement and then motioned with her hands to continue and not stop. He grinned and continued—. My father stayed with us in the Philippines for a few months. We travelled to numerous paradisiacal locations in Southeast Asia at that time. He then proposed to my mother and effortlessly persuaded her to immigrate to Canada.

He considered settling in Ottawa since he believed there were better opportunities for him to find a secure employment. Sadly, it was the circumstance —Sandra's face was puzzled and curious at the same time in response to his comment, but she decided not to question him—. My grandfather, Arthur Smith, the ex former prime minister of Canada, had a difficult relationship with my father. My dad chose to join the merchant marine not only because he enjoyed travelling but also to prevent my grandfather from trying to control his life, as he did with his older sister, my aunt Lena. Their relationship was not the best; they rarely spoke to one another. His father wanted him to pursue a profession in law or any field that would prepare him for entering politics; he hoped to his son be as prime minister himself someday. When my father saw how difficult and depressing his dear sister's life was, he realised that leaving that place would be the wisest course of action. He made the decision to relocate at the west of the country and enrol in the prestigious British Columbia Institute of Technology's nautical faculty.

As soon as we got to Ottawa, my parents married; they held an intimate wedding that barely twenty guests attended. Then my father asked my aunt Lena to help him get a job. Knowing well the profile of her brother and his remarkable ability with numbers, she recommended him to the Office of the Auditor General of Canada. When they knew that it was the son of Arthur Smith, he was immediately accepted, although my father was never aware of that fact.

Because of his fear of flying, most of his travels for work involved trains, which meant that he frequently spent extended amounts of time away from home. His employment involved inspecting various government departments across Canada. He needed some time, but he eventually became accustomed to his job. But due to his self-blocking attitude to learn technology, he was unable to develop in that government post.

When he was at home, he always made plans to share with the family, I remember. He frequently planned weekend excursions to locations in other provinces, regardless of the scheduling limitations. He appeared to be trying to make up for his absence. We relished that way of life, but as time went on, we noticed how worn out my father was. My mother says that she didn't learn the variables that, in her perspective, caused that dreadful disease until it was too late. According to my mother, the diagnosis he received was the result of him leaving his beloved life at sea so abruptly, working the same job for fourteen years without ever being promoted, stress brought on by his technological limitations, and the lengthy travel seasons in which he missed being at home. But what set off the incident was when Peter Hole, his former assistant and best friend, told him a painful truth.

After many years, Peter got in touch with him and expressed his desire to visit him. His friend travelled from Vancouver to see my dad, who was at that time in Ottawa. That reconnection, which brought back happy memories of his time as a sailor, really touched my father. He wanted to welcome him to his home, but his friend insisted that they meet somewhere else.

When the meeting day finally came, my father went directly from his job to the hotel restaurant where Peter was staying. They gave one other a warm hug and immediately started talking about everything that had happened to them while they had been apart. At first, the conversation was nice, full of stories, recollections, and laughs. But Peter suddenly took a serious stance and revealed to his friend that he had a heart attack six months prior and had even had a clinical death diagnosis when, to everyone's shock, he suddenly came back to life. Although he said to have little memory of the events surrounding his apparent death, he did recall feeling as though he was in a trance and had never previously felt a sense of serenity like that. He explained to him how that experience had transformed his life for the better, and how he had since committed himself to finding a way to have that mystical experience once more.

In addition to being unaware that his friend had been in danger of passing away, my father was astounded by the tremendous transformation he noticed in someone who had, to put it mildly, always been so shallow.

Peter continued by telling him about himself. He said he had joined a transcendental meditation group and was fully committed to his personal growth, but that every time he tried to move forward, something in his mind would get in the way. It was like a guilty feeling that kept him from finding the peace he was looking for. That's how he remembered the name of his best friend, Glem Smith, while digging through his memories. He then made the decision that they should get together again so that he could tell him a secret.

My father was initially as shocked as he was confused by those statements, but being the patient guy that he was, he chose to refrain from interjecting and waited for the conclusion of that tale.

Peter said again what he always said that he thought of him as more than just a friend, the older brother he never had, and that everything he did was because he thought it was in some way beneficial to him, but now that he could see things differently, he told him that, for that time, he was naive and manipulated.

He informed him that he had been my grandfather's informant for a while and had come to visit him because he felt agitated. The great Arthur Smith encouraged Peter to provide him a periodic account of my father's activities because, as the son of a well-known former Prime Minister, he desired to be informed of his son's actions in order to avoid having his name soiled. Peter described how my father's behaviour altered after he met my mother on the visit to the Philippines. Because of this, and as a result of a far higher command —influenced by my grandfather—, the ship they were assigned to abruptly altered its course from Asia to South America.

He also brought up several other instances where my father had said he was perplexed as to why some of his superiors' judgements didn't follow a logical course of action. He added that he called my grandfather and happily gave him all the information so that he could get in touch with my father and help promote this reunion. My grandfather congratulated him for their years of collaboration with, but he also mentioned that now that his son worked for the government, it was simpler for him to keep an eye on his activities.

Peter profusely apologised to his friend, saying that because of his youth, he was susceptible to being duped and used as a pawn by someone as skilled as my grandfather. What my father was hearing made him unable to believe it. Many things made obvious to him right away. He just decided to ask how much he had received for that treachery after a few awkward minutes of quiet and an expression of extreme sadness. Peter answered that the politician would occasionally send him gifts, which were typically scale models of sports cars, which were his hobby at the time, but he never received single money from his father or anybody else since, he was persuaded that he was acting in the best interests of the Smith family. At that point, the conversation came to an end. Without even saying goodbye to his former best friend, my father left the location.

He chose to walk the twenty-one kilometres between the hotel and the house that day to clear his head, so he arrived late at home. He missed work the following day and called in sick. He stated that he intended to leave that government job after telling my mum the entire tale. Even yet, he understood it wasn't the best choice because a 62-year-old guy with only one line of work —merchant seaman— would not have many prospects in the capital city's job market. In addition, he felt trapped in that position because of the house's mortgage and the trust he established to cover my tuition and other fixed costs.

My mother made an effort to persuade him to launch their own business. She proposed a Filipino restaurant or a language school, but nothing made him feel better. It appeared as though he had given up trying to combat his father and how he felt about his job. After that, he received a pancreatic cancer diagnosis in less than a year, and it took him only six months to pass away, exactly in the month that we graduated from high school. I didn't go because of that, and since you were the honour roll student next to me, you had the honour of speaking to the students at the ceremony.

My hero was my dad. He gave me all the skills I have; he passed on his love of exploration and travel, and I inherited his interests in literature and history. He served as a model for how to truly love a family by laying down his life for them.

Sandra was looking at Glem when he had done telling his tale, her green eyes welling up with tears. He wiped her cheeks clean of the tears with a cotton napkin. The restaurant was nearly empty and about to close at that point. He motioned for the bill, but she stopped him and spoke.

—You are my guest tonight, so don't worry; leave it alone —Sandra spoke in a lovely tone—. I'm grateful that you were honest with me and shared such a personal experience since it has helped me to understand a lot more.

—I am the one who must thank you for insisting; I feel as if I have unloaded a load of a ton of weight —answered Glem with an evident countenance of relief.

Glem had finished his training in the library in less than a month. It was not difficult for him to accomplish that achievement because he frequently visited the location and was a very smart youngster. He was highly at ease at work; he enjoyed visiting and conversing with the lawmakers that worked at that government building. His charisma and enthusiasm quickly made him quite well-liked by many who frequented the location.

After a few months passed, a situation led an unusually high number of lawmakers to begin visiting the library in search of resources to help them make judgements and act. In October 2001, Afghanistan has become embroiled in conflict. To remove the Taliban regime and destroy the Al Qaeda terrorist network, the United States and a handful of allies had invaded that nation. The Canadian government had to state its stance on the conflict diplomatically. As for Glem, he knew that there existed a tumultuous geopolitical world far beyond the comprehension of a simple twenty-year-old librarian. However, despite this, certain questions continued to swirl in his mind. Is humanity inevitably destined to repeat cycles of devastation and reconstruction? Will we ever truly become conscious of past mistakes and avoid repeating them? How will society learn to live in true harmony, or will this idea remain a grand utopia? The young man, whose passions included studying history, couldn't understand why leaders continued to fall into the error of using war to resolve conflicts, which inevitably became more painful than any other possible alternative.

He believed that the world could evolve in well-being to the extent that everyone on the planet achieved self-realization. He thought back to an important lesson he had learned as a child at that precise moment. One day, as he entered his father's study, he discovered a square of wood, about twelve inches on each side, with a small piece of rope attached. This rope was a thin sailor's rope, known in Spanish as "Piola," and it was made up of five twisted strands. This rope's open end had delicately split braids that each finished in a polished copper plate with a message carved in lovely Gothic-style letters on it. Each word represented one of the values his father considered essential to cultivate: Passion, Innovation, Originality, Leadership, and Abilities (PIOLA). He told the little boy that each human being should identify his own, because values are like the stars that guide man while he navigates in a turbulent world. Those words penetrated deep into the boy to the point that he decided to honor his father, cultivating those same values in his life.

He interacted with several lawmakers more frequently because of their increased library visits. Conversations frequently turned to the young man's fascinating points of view about how he interpreted the state of the world, its causes, and its effects, and his ideas were frequently praised by lawmakers.

On the other hand, having access to all the books that was one of the benefits of working there. Although they were unable to borrow any books, staff may always consult any books that were present. Glen had a strange and inquisitive mentality; therefore, he always chose to visit the library's "Rare Collection," which was a collection of books that didn't fall into any predetermined categories.

When he was reviewing that section one day, he found himself curiously drawn to a book. He hadn't read his title yet, but it felt as though the book had a magnetic pull on him. He inexplicably felt that the book would transform his life once it was in his hands, so he did not object and proceeded to take it.

CHAPTER II

FIRST TRAVEL

*"The most important thing in any area of life is to seek balance,
because the extremes are always harmful,
therefore an open mind and without prejudice
it will always be the best instrument to achieve our dreams"*

The book was roughly six inches broad by nine inches high, with a firm olive-green cover that has been extensively used and nearly three hundred yellowed pages that suggested it had not recently been issued. The title "The Quantum Machine" was displayed on its cover in raised letters that appeared to have once been golden due to the scant remnants of that colour.

The publisher and author's pages had been torn out, as if someone didn't want the identity of the author or publisher of that mysterious text to be revealed. In addition, the book wasn't presented as a science fiction story at all, but rather as a kind of comprehensive guide for building and using a curious time machine. Complementing this knowledge with in-depth discussions of quantum physics, cosmic phenomena, and an intriguing dissertation on time's none-linearity, the anonymous author of the book, argues for the existence of multiple realities that coexist simultaneously and the possibility of time travel. He also provided a thorough philosophical study of the relationship between the three components of a being —the body, soul, and mind—, and how rigorous training might help someone achieve the long-held goal of time travel.

Since then, the boy has tried to arrive at the library well before the start of his shift and stay there for several more hours, absorbed in that reading. He finds it not only fascinating but continually challenges his intelligence and imagination to the fullest. The discovery of that book caused the boy to drastically change his daily routine. After eating the book in a short period of time, he made the decision to read it again, but this time to take detailed notes and see if all the elements he had described were indeed possible. This is how, with incredible dedication, he started to put all the preparation techniques into practice so that he could attempt to carry out such a spectacular journey. This training included intense meditations, endless repetitions of enigmatic mantras spoken in a tongue he had never heard before, a strict vegan diet, and strenuous physical exercise; all of these were done with the intention of conditioning the body in an integral way in order to accomplish such a lofty goal.

The development of the quantum machine that would be his vehicle was another difficult assignment that Glem had to handle at the same time. The design and production of the quantum machine were meticulously detailed throughout the worn-out text's yellowed pages.

That special equipment might be made flawlessly by hand. Fortunately, the young guy had a special aptitude for working with his hands —another priceless bequest from his father—. He has spent many hours with him creating scale wooden boats since he was a boy. They have also created little sleds out of wood, among other things, including fishing rods they used when visiting several Canadian lakes.

In terms of the artefact, it was a four-sided pyramid with perfectly fitting wooden edges at each of its vertices, like a large puzzle as the construction was unable to accommodate a metallic component. The pyramid's faces were made of mirrors facing inward, and they were expertly assembled so that the union of their profiles was almost imperceptible. However, it was the precise installation of these, involving a laborious process of sanding, assembling, disassembling, re-sanding, and reattaching them repeatedly that caused the young perfectionist the most inconvenience, to the point where he wondered whether it was worth it. When the mirrors were set up and projected against each other from the inside, they created a beautiful illusion of endless depth. The base was a square of polished wood that had been painted matte black. A strong transparent nylon thread that was designed to lift the upper portion of the pyramid from the inside and was assembled as a single piece descended from the upper vertex of the 164 cm tall geometric figure after embracing a sturdy wooden beam that served as a pulley. This allowed access to and exit from this structure.

The handcrafted device was exquisite and had outstanding finishes. It was the product of long hours spent in the house's attic, during which his mother often complained about the constant noises he produced at odd hours of the night while she was unconscious of what was going on. But in the end, Glem's sense of fulfilment was huge and well deserved because, in order to conceal this enormous undertaking, he chose to complete all the construction work alone.

But even after a protracted time of rigorous physical and mental conditioning had passed, and despite having performed such great work, there was still a restlessness that consumed him.

A single component was required for the enigmatic ceremony that was mentioned in that document; it was a specific tree bark whose function was to put the person into an altered state that would enable him to complete the spectacular adventure. Although the young man could boast of his extensive knowledge of botany, which he had used on numerous trips along Canadian trails, this book introduced him to a new name, and although his research had shown that there were potential alternatives, the fact that he lacked absolute security caused him to question whether he would be able to accomplish his goal.

On one occasion, he was watching over a group of guests who were taking a tour of the library; towards the conclusion of the tour, a friendly old man emerged from the crowd, walked up to him, and spoke.

—When the pupil is ready, the master enters, —and he instantly hands him a small paper bag that contains an unknown item.

—Thank you so much for your kind gesture, sir —Glem remarked, startled by the sudden gesture. While attempting to return the parcel, he concluded—. That since it is a pleasure for us to serve you, the present is not necessary.

—Son, I assure you that keeping the items in this bag are in your best interests! —the elderly man replied, gesturing with his hands that he would not accept her return before going on to say—. Mya has told me a lot about you, and during my meditations, the ancestors directed me to give you a few pieces of bark from the sacred tree. I am the chief of the Cree village to whom Mya belongs —he adjusted his hat before bidding farewell—. It was a pleasure to meet you, and I was really taken by the zeal with which you go about your business. I wish you much success in all your endeavours. We might cross paths again!

After finishing his sentence, the elderly guy left the area, leaving Glem pale since he was unable to imagine where he would find the necessary ingredient to perform the ceremony in such an odd manner. The boy, who had no superstitions at all, was unable to come up with a rational explanation for that peculiar incident. He sought out his good friend Mya almost reflexively as a means of answering the troubling question that had just been raised. As he approached her, still a little perplexed, he said.

—Hello Mya, Glad to have found you! I want to tell you that I just met an elderly man —his companion then interrupts and speaks next.

—My dear boy, I am aware of the meeting you had with our revered leader, and also of your reaction. I can only tell you that in the world we inhabit, not everything is black or white since there is endless nuances that make us up. The most important thing in any area of life is to seek balance because extremes are always harmful, that's why an open mind and without prejudices will always be the best instrument to achieve dreams —concluded the pleasant lady with undeniable wisdom, resuming her work.

The young man thanked him for the advice and realised right away that having the right frame of mind was crucial to being able to complete his adventure. He then made a commitment to himself to carry out diligent inner work, doing everything in his power to reduce the intensity of his analytical mind so that he could accept the course of events with real amplitude.

After that, the boy decided it was time to verify all of the claims made in the book. Yet he began to be plagued by a series of persistent thoughts: Where to go? When in the past? Who should I go see? How could he make those journeys more useful for identifying the big questions?

He immediately recalled two points expressed in the book. First, it was said that any expedition should have a high purpose because the journey would not be accomplished if the traveller was unable to fully tune in with the pure energy of the cosmos. However, the text stated that any attempt to change an event in the past would result in the immediate interruption of the trip because the cosmos does not allow changes. The book provides a clear and in-depth explanation of a particular variant of the phenomenon known as the "butterfly effect", which allows demonstrating how any action could be enhanced a thousand times through the tunnel of time.

Conscious of these significant aspects and armed with all the elements to embark on his first adventure, the only thing missing was to define where to go. It was at that moment, unexpectedly, that the peculiar small wooden board resting in his father's study came back to his mind, where those five precious values could be observed. So he thought, 'What if I go in search of influential figures from the past who, in my opinion, represent each of those qualities and at the same time allow me to experience certain transcendental events of humanity?' Immediately, he searched his mind for someone who could best represent a quality like passion —which was the first of those five words—, and who had also witnessed crucial moments in history. The name of a very significant figure came to him.

The choice had already been made, so he spent days ensuring the meeting that had occurred in his mind. However, this question was far from simple, as the definition of the historical moment one wished to reach could not be determined by a specific date of some calendar, but rather corresponded to a strong alignment with the prevailing emotion at the historical moment one wanted to travel to, or, alternatively, the one experienced by the character whom one wanted to visit, in some space of his life.

THE PASSION

After much preparation, the night of the ritual finally arrived. It was eleven past eleven on a chilly Thursday in February, and a brilliant full moon could be seen through the attic's clean windows.

He entered the pyramid completely naked after a 12-hour fast, sat in a meditation position on a small but supportive black cushion, and then used a transparent nylon thread to manipulate the pyramid's top so that it rested on the base's uniquely designed channels, which allowed light to enter from the outside. He then started chanting a sequence of mantras, which served as a timer for when to drink the infusion created from that tree bark from a glass container. As he immersed himself in the ritual, he noticed that he was gradually falling into a state of trance. After an ambiguous period passed, he realised that he had successfully forced his consciousness to leave his body. Suddenly, the vision of endless mirrors had changed into a maze of corridors and doors. He had to use his intuition to figure out the corridor and portal that would take him to his goal after his entity had gained access to these.

The youngster became progressively agitated because of his lack of expertise in that circumstance and the variety of possibilities that were presented to him. He suddenly recalled that the book had always advised that in such situations it was essential to placate ideas and give closer attention to feelings. In this way, as soon as he focused all his emotions on passion, he noticed how his astral body moved into one of the passages. As he moved forward, he sensed a type of attraction to specific doors, but he wasn't sure enough of it to know which one was the right one. He suddenly noticed a translucent figure in front of one of them that reminded him of the elderly native guy he had met a few weeks earlier. Then he remembered when the old man had said, «We might cross paths again!» at that same moment he put all of his effort on going back there and passing through that door.

Going through it, he saw something unexpected right away: his entire body was like a flawless hologram, and even as emotions filled him, he felt as though they controlled his entire being and warped reason. His five senses were numb, but he could hear the various sounds around him, albeit very faintly.

His ethereal body magically arrived in front of the stairs of a small but lovely house at that precise time as he focused all his emotion on the selected character. The house was perfectly aligned with many other similarly constructed homes. A lot of horse-drawn carriages were driving through the neighbourhood, which had cobblestone streets, rows of lit oil lamps, and nicely dressed residents wearing overcoats and hats.

He made up his mind to go into that house and was amazed to find that he could walk through the doors as if he were a ghost. When he entered, he was pleasantly surprised by the exquisite design of the space. The most beautiful item in that room was a huge portrait of a woman wearing a courtesan outfit, and beside saw some long-necked decanters that were sitting on a plain sideboard, and right away, he saw him. About five years old, he was a very nice boy with white skin, well coiffed straight black hair, a slim physique, and bright blue eyes who was dressed very neatly. While waiting for his mother to get ready to go, the boy, reacted by releasing a lovely round music box he was holding in his hands and shifting his focus to the fireplace as if he had just become aware of the visitor who had just entered the house. Glem remained standing while waiting to see if he could be seen. The child extended his left hand in welcome without exhibiting any sign of anxiety. He then picked up the ornament once again and began toying with it while waiting for the nice lady to call. The young man was aware that his presence could be felt as soon as he entered the home.

However, despite not understanding why he had gone to meet that personality when he was a youngster, the traveller was able to flow through the events because he was aware that everything had a purpose.

In a stunning beige cashmere coat that she had just put on, the mother addressed the creature at that same moment as she emerged from her room.

—Son, get up and wrap up well, we must leave immediately because the carriage will arrive soon —after saying that she suddenly developed an intense coughing fit that made her uncomfortable.

—I'm ready, mommy —answered the little boy, who excitedly jumped out of his seat, picked up his jacket and ran to meet him.

After hearing the conversation, Glem was once more taken aback by how easy he could record people's thoughts while they spoke, reducing the need to listen to their voices, which he could nonetheless faintly hear.

He quickly became aware that he was exiting the carriage alongside the lovely woman and her young child. These were travelling toward a major neighbourhood. When they were close enough, they hurried to open a side door that was only meant for staff entry. It was a music-hall in the heart of London.

That lovely woman performed there as a singer and actress. And when she got there, she was all set to take the stage. When her son saw mom working behind the scenes, he showed a great deal of admiration by keeping his sky-blue eyes open wider than usual.

When she attempted to hit a high note in the middle of her performance, she experienced a coughing fit once more, but this time it became so severe that she had to leave the stage. As a sign of unhappiness, the crowd started to grumble, and the noise level grew louder and louder. The woman was being severely reprimanded by the property owner behind closed doors. She excused herself by saying that she was powerless to stop it.

The infant was watching everything that was going on and shifted his eyes to the corner where the young's hologram was positioned.

—I must do something —said speaking to Glem.

—Just go with the flow and follow your heart —almost intuitively, the young man responded mentally.

After smiling in response to the advice, the boy ran toward the stage. During all that utter turmoil, a young child's voice was heard singing a cappella the same hymn that his mother had just finished singing. The audience was transfixed by the young boy's sweet and well-tuned voice, and just as he reached the verse where the singer had stopped, he jokingly started to cough purposely, as if to suggest that this was part of the arrangement. The audience erupted in laughter and applause at that precise moment, the theatre owner and the actress were baffled by the unplanned performance, and young Charles Chaplin experienced for the first time the enthusiasm that would follow him throughout his entire artistic career. He thought, «Now I know what I want to do for the rest of my life» as he bowed before the audience.

The traveller was taken aback when he suddenly felt the same intensity of passion and feeling as the aspiring artist, confirming the close bond he had been able to forge with the chosen person.

Another aspect that equally impacted the young man was recognizing how, in that state, he could express phrases and ideas charged with a philosophical depth, which was far from the experience of a twenty-year-old. At that moment he understood what the book was referring to, when he affirmed that the part of the being that made the journey was his timeless mind, which had no beginning or end, and which remained continuously connected to universal wisdom. Thanks to this elevated state of consciousness and prior knowledge of the life of the chosen character, the traveler felt a certain freedom to be able to interact with him, without fear of interfering during events in the past.

While Glem was still blissfully savouring that sensation, he suddenly noticed how his subtle consciousness floated, returning to the same passageway full of doors where he had first begun the journey. This time, though, with greater assurance, he was able to recognise the portal that most attracted him, and without any assistance, he stopped and crossed that threshold with complete determination.

Unexpectedly, he found himself in an elegant living room that had been tastefully decorated in the English style of the middle of the nineteenth century. The large room was covered in a lovely carpet, some author paintings, mostly depicting beautiful European landscapes, were displayed on the wide walls, and elegant mahogany furniture served as the backdrop for an interesting meeting. About twelve-year-old Chaplin was enjoying a delightful conversation with a very dapper and attractive man. The traveller quickly learned that he had coincided with the future comedian's first official theatre role from a well-known British actor, screenwriter, and director.

—The script for Sammy's role is here, boy —that eloquent man spoke while gesturing for those in the room to come meet the boy—. You should be aware that this is one of my comedy's most significant roles.

—I appreciate you giving me this chance, my lord. I swear I won't disappoint you! —the young boy responded while bowing his head in appreciation to everyone observing him—. Once I go home, I'd like to carefully go over the papers —due to his poor reading ability and concern over being discovered, Charles ended nearly as if making a request.

—Son, of course! —with a friendly smile, the man responded—. We will soon let you know the time and location of the rehearsals.

The small boy exited the "Green Room", a prominent artists' club, feeling an emotion beyond words. He regularly glanced to his right as he walked, recognizing that the Glem entity that was with him on the journey shared the elation that was gushing at that very moment with him.

The young man was already daydreaming about his life as a dedicated actor while riding the lengthy bus ride home on that wet London afternoon. He struck up a conversation with his particular travelling buddy at that precise moment.

—I must prepare myself thoroughly since I cannot afford to miss this opportunity, which I have long yearned for —he spoke as he clasped his fingers together as though in prayer—. I know my brother will have the time to help me memorise my lines because I'd be lost without him! To become a great actor, I must improve my reading skills.

—The secret to success in life is believing in your abilities and working tirelessly —Glem replied briefly and concisely.

The traveller then saw a succession of events from the renowned actor's adolescence, as if it were a short film. He saw the excitement of his first works' debuts and rehearsals. The many weeks spent touring across England's northern regions, where the young artist received the greatest salary possible, the public's sincere applause.

However, he also noticed instances where the boy, with tears in his eyes, questioned whether his mother —who was confined to a mental hospital for her recurrent episodes of dementia and who also suffered from malnutrition as a result of the family's poor living conditions— would have somewhat improved his condition.

He occasionally missed playing games with the neighbourhood boys and, of course, his elder brother Sydney, who had always been his unwavering adventure partner.

However, that boy was aware of two things that were equally important to him: first, that this life shielded him from returning to the orphanages where he had endured so much suffering; and second, that all those conflicting emotions magically disappeared when the curtain opened, and he was instantly transported to a parallel dimension full of beautiful emotions, where his skill and intelligence were fully expressed.

At the conclusion of that brief passage filled with happy and sad memories, Glem saw in the boy, because of the bond that had developed between them, a certain growth and, overall, a sense that he had managed to accept, with unusual maturity for his age, the pleasures and sacrifices that the thrilling and not always well-weighted career of acting entailed.

The traveller once more went through the motions that would put him at another period of that star's life. Because of the way people were dressed, the automobiles that were cruising the city's vast avenues, the warm weather, and the proximity to the sea, he quickly realised that he was not in Europe. It brought back memories that when Chaplin decided to risk starting his artistic career in the United States; it was in the famed film capital of Los Angeles, California.

It didn't take long for Glem to realise, when he felt a sudden chill run through his subtle body, that he was witnessing one of the greatest moments in the history of silent cinema, the creation of the character of Charlot, when he appeared on a recording set, around a beach known as Venice, which at the time was full of extras.

The fortunate young man was able to observe firsthand how that cinematic genius managed to develop such a paradoxical amusing character at the age of only twenty-four. As he consisted of a fun bum who always tried to behave like a gentleman, demonstrating good manners and a noble heart, however, his naivety and clumsiness of him would constantly cause him serious problems, from which he frequently managed to escape by appealing to his immense cunning. In this way, throughout this masterful interpretation, he was drawing endless laughter from the audience.

After the recording was complete, "Kid Auto Races at Venice," a memorable six-minute short film, was created.

Charles was confident that he had created a wonderful character, and though it was the result of his prodigious ingenuity, he acknowledged the significant contribution of four of his friends who helped create the bum's amusing wardrobe by providing him with the funny bulging pants, the little tailcoat, the extravagant shoes, and the bowler hat, as the actor's only personal belonging was his irreplaceable cane.

—I enjoy it and feel at ease in my character; my only concern is whether I will be able to express all my thoughts on stage —Chaplin stated as he awaited the young man's response.

—The potential for spectacular results when brilliance and diligence combine is boundless —the young man responded as if he were speaking to an old friend.

Charles sighed with relief, nodded, and carried out the remaining filming responsibilities.

Glem was shown the life of the famous artist once more, but this time he was pleasantly astonished to discover that he did not have to go back to the corridor of limitless doors to encounter the character at subsequent points in his life. This gave him the opportunity to see how, in the year that he made his Keystone Studios debut; he produced 35 short films, some of which he even directed. He was also impressed by how quickly his popularity spread and was appreciated, as he went from making only $150 per week at first to signing a record-breaking contract worth $1 million per year in just five years.

Suddenly, the traveler felt how the tour of those events stopped abruptly, discovering that he was during the First World War.

He saw firsthand how deftly the US government had used the star's fame to encourage him to support war bonds, which would be used to fund the nation's military and other necessities throughout the conflict.

—I have no reason to decline this country's request for assistance, to which I owe my professional success —Charles then began their usual telepathic exchange.

—Sincere gratitude is a key that opens innumerable doors and at the same time it is our best business card —was the boy's eloquent response.

But Chaplin would subsequently come to the conclusion that the country, and particularly its residents, suffered greatly as a result of the United States' choice to enter that war thousands of kilometres from its border. On the other hand, he gradually realised that it was political and financial interests rather than national security and sovereignty that prevented him from making that regrettable choice because they were never actually in threat. The power economy of the time, along with a group of influential politicians looking for leadership, chose the warmongering option due to the real risk that the member countries of the triple Entente made up of France, the United Kingdom, and Russia during the war, in the event of losing, would not be able to honour the debts acquired with the big New York banks.

As for Glem, prove his current anti-war stance by pointing out those more than one hundred thousand North American soldiers perished during the Great War, and that number triples if we include the injured and the mutilated. An increase in debt, inflation, and monetary changes contributed to the devastating phenomenon known as the Great Depression to emerge in the postwar period, which resulted in a terrible financial contraction without precedent. The health system was compromised due to the arrival from Europe of the so-called Spanish fever, which claimed the lives of about five hundred thousand people.

The change that brought the youngster to a new stage in the life of the prominent figure occurred after these sad occurrences had passed, and the boy experienced it as though it were a dizzying roller coaster ride. On this occasion, he attended a very formal evening that was held in a lavish theatre with high ceilings, excess ornamentation, enormous chandeliers that beautifully illuminated the space, everyone in attendance dressed to the nines, and the enormous number of journalists made him realise that it was a lavish event.

He learned that he was at the premiere of the popular film "City Lights," in which the multifarious artist was named as director, producer, screenwriter, musician, and starring actor, as soon as he tuned in to one of the journalists who was at the time writing a short press release. When he finally saw him, he was struck by an intriguing fact: Chaplin was joined by another legendary character who even managed to surpass him in terms of reputation. This person was none other than the renowned German physicist Albert Einstein. As he got closer to them, who were only a thought away, he overheard an excellent conversation.

—What I most admire about his art is its universality. You don't say a word and, nevertheless... The world understands it —commented the physicist with genuine admiration.

—It is true, but your merit is even greater! Well, everyone admires you, when no one understands a single word of yours —responded the artist with the genius that characterized him.

Everyone in attendance started laughing, and numerous reporters seized the chance to record that original speech. One of the journalists used the opportunity to ask the comedian a question.

—Tell me, Mr. Chaplin, if it is true that you asked Miss Virginia Cherrill to perform 342 takes of the same scene during the movie's filming! Because you were not happy with the outcome —asked that man with a shocked expression.

—The greatest risk of working beside me is that I am an obsessive perfectionist, which is well known to everyone —answered the actor with a tone more honest than arrogant.

That response was merely a testament to that genius' ability, as Glem recounted how, throughout his voyage through the star's life; he frequently saw instances in which the star gave the order to destroy a whole set because he did not like a particular detail. Additionally, they could occasionally stand in front of a recording set for hours or even days at a time waiting for a better idea to continue a movie without giving the least thought to the enormous sum of money that would be lost by postponing a movie at a Hollywood studio. The youngster appeared to be reflecting as he thought «Thanks to his passion and his gifts of genius, it is because in the North American silent film industry, all roads lead to Chaplin» and then he thought back to the moments, when he could marvel at how Charles had learned to play the violin and cello entirely on his own, having put in many hours of practise.

As he continued his trek, he once more encountered extremely gloomy circumstances. When World War II broke out, the government asked the comic once more to use his likeness to advertise the new war bonds, but this time the actor's response was unexpected.

—That's incredible! … Again, they ask me to assist them in selling their war papers —this is referencing the bonds—. However, I am no longer the same young man who began his profession in his twenties. Although I am tremendously appreciative of this nation, I also believe that I have more than paid it back. For a segment of society, in particular the government, I am the type of employee who must be instructed on what to do, think, and how to behave. My privacy has been destroyed, and I now resemble a circus animal. And what really cracks me up is how offended they become if I decline to play their jester —the actor argued with sincere regret—. But I've made the decision to remain out of it this time. I announce that I am an agent of peace!

—I'm afraid you've discovered the price of fame, which is none other than fame itself —was Glem's brief and brilliant response.

The traveller was once more able to sense the anguish and rage that overcame his interlocutor in his typical mood of empathy. Even more so, he realised a unique fact that completely corroborated the confession he had just heard. Contrarily, despite making innumerable movies that are regarded as masterpieces of the seventh art, that bright star has never won an Oscar for acting or directing during his filmography.

Now, returning to the matter of the war, the traveler witnessed how the character's refusal to support the government's warlike behavior led to accusations of communism and anti-American activities. The FBI was watching him, and although he was called to testify several times, he never showed up, claiming he had nothing to defend himself against. Not even the production of his movie "The Great Dictator," in which he brilliantly satirized Nazism and Hitler himself, was able to lessen the hostile treatment he received from the American judicial system.

After such distressing incidents had passed, Glem was overjoyed to see the peace of the years during his self-exile in Switzerland. He thoroughly liked seeing his last four films come to fruition as he used to; and by experiencing it firsthand, he was able to feel the artist's huge emotion upon receiving the twelve-minute ovation during the well-deserved honorary Oscar in Los Angeles at the age of eighty-three years.

Then Glem had the impression of travelling to the famous actor's lovely Swiss country residence, as if his intangible body were a kite. He hears an address once he enters the grand main room.

—Thank you, my enigmatic friend! For being there with me during the most significant events in my life. —this time, the youngster was being addressed by an intangible image of Chaplin who was slowly vanishing into the room's corners like mist.

—Thank you, my dear master, for your invaluable teachings and your magnificent legacy. I don't know how to describe the immense pleasure that it brought me to meet you and to live by your side through the tumultuous events that transformed the course of humanity —was Glem's response, moved by that sublime moment.

Thus, at the age of eighty-eight, the idol's life came to an end on a chilly Christmas morning, along with the extraordinary voyage of the traveller.

THE CONFERENCE

As soon as he regained consciousness, he noticed two startling facts: first, this return journey had gone admirably quickly and smoothly in comparison to the beginning of his odyssey, and secondly, he found that as he lifted the top part of the pyramid and stepped out of it, he was astonished to see that the large clock with hands, strategically positioned on the column in front of the quantum machine, It showed 1:11 AM. At that moment, he realized the entire process —which had felt like an eternity— had only taken him two hours to complete. At that point, he was able to comprehend the complex explanations of space-time notions made in the book, which paraphrased Albert Einstein's own theories, this time from personal experience.

Still agitated by the trip, he felt very thirsty, as if he had just run a full marathon without stopping, so he got dressed and went down to the kitchen, at that moment on the stairs he ran into his mother, who was already preparing to retire to her room.

—Good night, son, and get some sleep. I beg you not to make any noise today; I need to rest because I'm worn out —she spoke to him while giving him a bear hug and a tender kiss, but Ada noticed how her body began to shiver with an intense and incomprehensible sensation—, what is happening to you, son?

—I was just exercising, and that's why I'm a little agitated, mama —the youngster responded fast to avoid providing an explanation, but at that same time he realized, surprised, the strength of the energy field he was capable of dispersing after doing such an unusual activity.

Following that adventure, Glem continued to experience intense thrill. It seemed as though he had emotional inertia from the travel because every time he thought back on an incident, he experienced it all over again, not just in his mind but with every fibre of his body. At that moment he thought «It's time to channel all this powerful energy»

He decided that the best way to go about it would be to tell others about his fascinating experience, without, of course, going into detail about how he learned such important knowledge.

Using his impressive storytelling abilities, he set to work and prepared an original conference in which he made an informed analysis of the causes and effects of the most significant events of the first half of the 20th century through the eyes of the North American film industry, and of course its most prominent representative.

He initially tried out the fascinating conversation, which lasted for nearly an hour, with his friends and fellow librarians, doubtless including the highly enlightened Mrs. Trembley. The feedback from this first focus group was outstanding; everyone praised the excellent details that had been provided as well as the captivating manner in which they had been conveyed, the flawless timeline of events, and, above all, the very authentic decision to use cinema, and in particular Chaplin's life, as the masterful thread that had led the narrative of those remarkable events of the previous century. Glem confirmed that this was the best plan he could come up with to manage the emotionality he continued to feel following the trip.

Already feeling more confident as a result of those inspiring words, he started presenting the conference in all the locations that were ready to host it at that point. He went to the church where her mother gave language classes, capturing the interest of the young people there and having them appreciate the stories as if they were mighty fictional tales. Then, he addressed to his old high school, and he did two conferences that received positive feedback from both the student body and the board. In fact, the latter voluntarily extended a number of letters of recommendation addressed to other high schools in the city so that he could give his fascinating talk there.

For this reason, once he felt more confident, he decided to get in touch with his aunt Lena once more and try to contact to certain colleges and institutions in the province through her. After receiving the request, the ever-diligent minister did the appropriate action, and the youngster was soon touring several colleges and universities across the enormous province of Ontario.

The young man unexpectedly received the honour of being asked by the University of Ottawa to show his work in that prestigious venue. Up until that point, he had managed to gain some notoriety within that educational environment, particularly due to the uniqueness of the content of his talk and the extraordinary way he handled and shared information.

The long-awaited day finally arrived, and Glem was taken to the main campus auditorium. Its capacity of just over three hundred seats was full, with high-ranking authorities of the renowned institution occupying the first two rows of central seats while curious students from various faculties filled the remaining seats to see if the positive comments made about the young man and his original presentation were accurate.

The crowd erupted in ovation that lasted for several minutes after an emotional performance of eighty minutes. When the eagerly anticipated question and answer session finally arrived, a young woman from the audience took the mic and addressed the speaker.

—I want to congratulate you for your fascinating presentation! But I'm curious as to how you were able to compile such exact and thorough information on the persons and incidents you mention. You seemed to speak as though you had experienced those events and interacted with all those people! —asked the girl, truly interested.

—The fact is, fortunately, I do not possess Dorian Gray's gifts! —a few in the audience laughed since they were familiar with the legendary author Oscar Wilde's masterwork as the young man responded brilliantly—. I must admit that I developed a love of reading, and I was able to obtain materials in various languages that allowed me to complete the information I just gave you —Glem utilized this deftly prepared response to escape from trouble.

Then came a string of significant questions, all of which the guy expertly responded to. But as the meeting came to a close, a well-known figure from the audience requested to speak.

—I have a few questions I would like to ask —that interlocutor asked in an arrogant manner—, Could you tell us why Chaplin fled to Switzerland? Does this action validate his communist tendencies? Well, his acquaintance with Hollywood blacklister composer Hanns Eisler was clear, and what can be said about communists Pablo Picasso and Gromyko, the Soviet chancellor? He might have wished to avoid the tax evasion allegations that the US government was looking into at the time. Not to mention the scandals that resulted in his marriages to minors, which would later lead to contentious divorces, possibly prompted by his promiscuous behavior given that it is estimated that he had close to two thousand lovers —a succession of whispers permeated the room as that arrogant young man concluded.

—Appreciate Enzo Rizzi. I'll do my best to respond based on the knowledge I have. However, I must admit that it appears to me that your sources are vanity publications! —Glem spoke with the assurance of someone who had been a remarkable eyewitness to those events, and he took pleasure in watching as the murmurs turned to derisive laughter at his astute comment—. Chaplin had countless friends, from almost any political doctrine, race, or religion, but he was only labeled for his friends associated with communism. Allow me to cite an interesting anecdotal fact, it is said that the FBI placed microphones in his house, but the recordings did not reveal anything significant, as they only captured long sessions of silence, as if it were one of his movies. It is especially ironic that time has proven this character right; as many people agree that his solid pacifist stance helped him become the legend he is today. They even claim that all the advice and phrases he left for posterity are undeniably truthful and relevant, something we cannot affirm of many politicians and personalities who opposed him in his time.

If the tax evasion allegations are accurate, I believe he would be the first individual to avoid the US Internal Revenue Service and return to US soil without being detained or penalised because he was allowed to do so when invited to accept his famous honorary Oscar. Additionally, his wife returned to Los Angeles immediately after living in Switzerland, and without any hindrance, she sold all the artist's possessions.

Regarding his first two brides were both sixteen years old when they got married, which is true, but each time, their parents gave their consent for the union to go through. About his three divorces, I'll say that the tabloids oversaw sensationalising the facts and violating the privacy of everyone concerned. I think there were no winners in those sad battles, other from the media, of course.

Finally, I'll be honest and say that I have no way of knowing if the number of lovers you suggest is accurate, possibly because I never thought that kind of frivolity related to my research. I hope I've been able to allay your doubts with this. I don't know if perhaps at this moment some late-night entertainment journalist, taking advantage of technology, is aiming new questions in your ear, but if not, I would like to conclude this talk here, which has become somewhat longer than usual —the audience erupted in cheers at the conclusion of his speech, and Enzo, who had been irritated by the loud answers he had received and the mocking but accurate reference Glem had made to his conduct during the interview, vanished into the crowd.

After a short while, the young man went back to his normal routine, but he was excited about the prospect of going on a new trip because he remembered that there would soon be another full moon. In his mind, the names of other characters were already circulating, which, in his opinion, accurately represented the words that were still left to be said. He then started making careful preparations for his upcoming trip through time.

CHAPTER III

INVENTION AND ORIGINALITY

"Friends are the family we choose,
and instead of blood ties,
we are joined by ties of love,
that can be easily damaged if not taken care of"

Before the perfect time to start his next adventure arrived, Glem set out to reread the book, paying close attention to a section that described what it would be like to start a voyage in the past and by deliberate control of their emotions, might at will travel to a different time or location or meet a specific individual. This comprehensive description made more sense to him at that precise moment because of his first experience. So, in order to cultivate such a unique talent, the book suggested using some acting-related principles so as to be able to channel emotions and use them as a compass, which would allow the traveler to wander freely across many eras of time.

The talented young man had participated in the school's theatre program during his final two years, and it was precise while performing in Shakespeare's well-known play "Othello" that he first became good friends with Sandra, who played the part of Desdemona, the protagonist's wife, in that theatrical tragedy filled with profound rhetoric. Without a second thought, he proceeded to meet her valued friend, whom he had invited to a meeting at one of his favorite locations, the restaurant "The Green Door."

Sandra, I'm so happy you're here! You remain as attentive as always —in this manner, Glem, who was already there, welcomed her companion and gave her a warm hug—. Please sit down. Would you want some tea?

Of course! A cinnamon tea would be nice, thanks —she responded less enthusiastically than her buddy—. Although I'm more interested in finding out what you're doing right now. Because we haven't spoken in a while, when we do cross paths during shift changes, I constantly notice you engrossed in that enigmatic book. Do you wish to memorize it? —she said reproachfully.

—Don't say you're jealous of a book —the boy responded while laughing.

—You're aware that it's not jealousy —she kept claiming him—. Because everyone around you is a little concerned, and because I know you well enough to know that you change once you are enthusiastic about something, it is unusual that you haven't informed me or the others anything about this. Remember that Friends are the family we choose, and instead of blood ties, we are joined by ties of love, that can be easily damaged if not taken care of.

—Worried? Who? Why? —his face went from laughing to wondering at that very instant.

—Several of your friends, Glem —the girl responded as if she were confessing—. You suddenly withdraw from everyone and spend all of your time reading the same book. You also radically altered your diet; I know you have always eaten well, but you were never a vegan. They overheard you speaking incoherently odd words when you were by yourself. Your mom says you shut yourself up and work till the break of day on a mysterious project. Tell me Glem, are you into some strange religion?

—You can relax, friend. Nothing further than that, I'm sorry if I came across as a little enigmatic. I assure you that I will explain my weird conduct to you soon —he tried to soothe his friend by speaking calmly—. I phoned you because I wanted to talk to you and ask if you still had the summary of the well-known Stanislavski book "An Actor Prepares," which we used back when we were studying theatre in school.

—Knowing you are still sane gives me peace of mind because your speaking tour and current interest in acting have truly helped to calm me down, I must wait patiently for you to reveal your new secret —the sweet young woman spoke, sighing with relief—. You know how organised I am, so yeah!, I still have that synopsis —proudly concluded.

That afternoon, they conversed as easily as they used to, laughed as they recalled some anecdotes, and even Glem suggested they go on a trip together to a small city 300 miles south of Ottawa in the province of Ontario. She said she would go along with him just as they had taken interesting walks together on other occasions.

As Glem held the book's summary in his hands —a must-read for any self-respecting actor— He was determined to master the methods the aforementioned Russian author had advised in order to effectively control and communicate the feelings and emotions shown in a script. As a result, he soon experienced a certain level of confidence, which allowed him to dare to travel through time to encounter two different characters in two separate eras. Even on this occasion, the choice of the first figure to visit in the past not only corresponded to the relationship it had with the word "Innovation," the second value on the small table, but also his analytical mind suggested that the selection should be strategic in order to assist in resolving a deep questioning that had arisen regarding whether all of that quantum experience was real or simply the product of a powerful hallucination induced by the sacred tree bark tea.

As the day of his second journey arrived, once again at eleven minutes past eleven on a spring night adorned with a breathtaking full moon, Glem embarked upon the enigmatic ritual that would lead him through endless corridors of infinite doors. His quest was to encounter the personalities that had already taken root in his mind. On this occasion, he felt a profound sense of comfort as he began his journey through time, finding it more fluid and comfortable than the first. Moreover, he effortlessly identified both the hallway and the correct portal, setting forth on his expedition with newfound ease.

Once he crossed the threshold, he beheld a breathtaking landscape: a radiant sun bathing an extensive green meadow, an elegant country mansion located next to a huge barn, where an imposing mill stood out, horses, carts, and a large group of workers performing their tasks. At that moment, simply by thinking it, Glem moved into the interior of the installation, where the mill was located. Inside, many people were engaged in various tasks, and among the crowd, two children of approximately ten years old ran chasing each other throughout the place. Suddenly, one of them, upon noticing the presence of the young man, stopped abruptly, accidentally stumbling over a wooden shelf and causing several empty containers to fall, resulting in a great commotion. Immediately, all those present turned to see what had happened, while Mr. Herdman, with an inquisitive look, peeked out from the window of his office to find out what was going on.

—Father, it was Aleck who did it! —cried a frightened Ben, pointing to his friend who had frozen in place at the scene of the incident, his gaze fixed on the spot where Glem's entity had been.

—Why don't you do something useful instead? We have a lot of work to do here, and I don't need any more setbacks —the owner of the place said sternly, addressing the young boys—. You two, clean up the mess and get back to work —he added, this time speaking to two workers who were standing nearby the shelf.

—Let's get out of here quickly, before things get worse! —Ben urged his friend in a rush.

—Just give me a moment, I want to ask your father something —Aleck replied, heading towards the busy gentleman's office.

—I don't know what you're trying to do, but I'll wait for you at the house —said Ben as he started to run towards the mansion.

As soon as the young boy entered the office, he took a deep breath and, armed with courage, spoke up.

—Excuse me, Mr. Herdman, I'd like to ask you a question —he said, standing in the doorway.

—Go ahead, my boy —replied the man, not taking his eyes off some papers on his desk.

—What's the most complicated job to do at the mill? —asked the curious boy, slowly walking towards the visitor's chair with the intention of sitting down.

—That's an interesting question, my dear little friend —the businessman said, this time fully focused on the child—. In this trade, the most complicated task is to remove the husk from the wheat, and then grind it into flour.

—Hmm, I understand! And could I see how that process is done? —the young boy asked again, expecting a positive response.

—I don't quite understand your interest, but if you want to know, ask the foreman to show you how it's done —Mr. Herdman concluded, waving him away from the office.

The excited boy sprang up from his seat and, turning towards the door, triumphantly raised his right arm in celebration of the response he had just received in front of the traveler, who stood a few meters away.

After meeting with the foreman and observing the procedure closely, the ingenious young boy knew that he could do something to improve the task at hand. So, at the end of the day, bidding farewell to his neighbor and best friend Ben, he headed home with a small sack full of wheat ears. As soon as he had finished his dinner, he locked himself in his father's shed to work on his idea.

After a week of long days of work and testing, which Glem witnessed and thoroughly enjoyed, he completed the fabrication of an innovative machine for threshing wheat. It consisted of several wooden paddles rotating together with a system of clove brushes, creating a device as simple as it was functional.

Thus, at the tender age of twelve, this character had built his first invention. Once he showed it to Mr. Herdman, who was greatly impressed, the gentleman addressed the young boy.

—I must confess, young man, you have truly surprised me! This device actually works! —exclaimed the gentleman, as he gave the boy gentle congratulatory pats on the back.

—Thank you, Mr. Herdman! I love creating things —replied the boy, his heart racing with excitement.

—Well, I'll tell you what, as a token of my appreciation for your hard work, I'll give you that small space and build you a workshop so you can continue inventing —said the always courteous man, pointing to a corner at the back of the barn where a small cubicle full of junk was located.

—Thank you so much, sir! I promise I'll create many useful things —replied the young boy, jumping for joy.

At that moment, the very young Alexander Graham Bell was obtaining the first of his many invention workshops.

During this new and exciting adventure, Glem was able to witness the future scientist from a young age. He perceived him as a reserved and even a bit introspective young man, but with a particular passion for music, to the point that he witnessed how he learned to play the piano on his own, being the only musician in that family, more oriented towards other disciplines such as speech and elocution.

It was always a pleasure to watch Aleck —as his family and friends called him—, entertains guests with his mimics and even some ventriloquism, when he felt comfortable, in his childhood home in Scotland.

Years later, the traveler witnessed how a young Bell managed to create a sign language in order to communicate with his mother, who suffered from degenerative hearing loss. It was precisely this circumstance that motivated him to study acoustics and speech therapy professionally.

However, it was when the entire family moved to the city of Brantford in Ontario, Canada, that Glem witnessed the most prolific stage of the renowned inventor.

In his new laboratory, in that wide and charming property on the banks of the Grand River, which included an orchard, a beautiful house, a stable, a chicken coop, and a carriage parking, one could appreciate the dedicated Bell immersed in his multiple studies on hearing and speech, coupled with his tireless work towards the creation of a multiple telegraph. But fate had a new change of course in store for him when Bell's father was contacted by a prestigious school for the deaf in Boston, Massachusetts, USA, in order to train instructors in sign language. He declined the offer and recommended his son instead, who by then was twenty-four years old.

—My father suggests that I take the job offer in the US, but I'm undecided. I enjoy teaching as much as inventing devices, but I'm unsure how long it would take me to set up a new laboratory elsewhere —spoke the scientist with hesitation. It was the first time he had engaged in a conversation with the traveler.

—For an inventor, the most valuable instrument is their ingenuity, which is why they will never start from scratch again. The experience of having once obtained the necessary resources for work is the greatest advantage when repeating that labor —Glem responded, his words imbued with the emotion that overwhelmed him at that moment.

Comforted by that conversation, Alexander Graham embarked on a phase of great growth in his life. With joy, Glem witnessed how that character became an extraordinary teacher, who also successfully applied his language therapy techniques to many students with hearing, speech, or both disabilities, with whom he often created a close friendly bond; just as it would happen with the famous deaf-blind speaker Helen Keller, who with great appreciation for her teacher, would express notable and heartfelt words, *"I thank you for your dedication to penetrate the inhuman silence that separates and strangles."* By then, the traveler also witnessed how love would arise between the distinguished professor and one of his deaf-mute students, a sublime union that would endure until the end of their days.

As for his tireless facet as an inventor, it was common to see him carrying the different artifacts he worked on every time he traveled to his home in Canada, thus never interrupting his creative activity. And precisely, it was on one of those trips that Glem —who longed to discover some data that would be useful to decipher the mystery of whether those time travels were entirely real—, found certain information that he deemed crucial. In this way, that young man with a special interest observed the numbering that the scientist assigned to the telephone apparatus that rested in his laboratory in Brantford Ontario, and relying on his good memory, memorized the number 1874072611, engraved on the underside of the wooden base, which would ultimately be the first functional telephone invented.

After that special moment, Glem was able to delve into the busy life of that famous figure, experiencing with excitement the first effective telephone communication in history.

—Hello, can you hear me? —thus began the conversation, the loyal assistant of Bell, who was in a room adjacent to the inventor's.

—Watson, come hither, for I must lay eyes upon thee —spoke his superior, riddled with curiosity as to whether his words had been fully apprehended.

The joy that all present felt —including Glem— upon seeing the faithful collaborator Thomas Watson appear in the room, manifesting that he had understood that order, was magnificent.

Then, the traveler witnessed, embraced the pride transmitted by the prolific inventor, the moment when the Bell Telephone Company was founded, in which Alexander Graham's father-in-law was a partner and the first president. He also accompanied him during the registration of his multiple patents in the United States and around the world, both for the first device and its continuous improvements. He witnessed the first long-distance telephone communication —which at that time was a meager six kilometers—, from the scientist's house to the telegraph office. The installation of the first public telephone in Hamilton, Ontario, Canada. The first transcontinental communication between New York and San Francisco. The continuous presentations of his emblematic invention to different personalities of his time, among which was the very Queen Victoria. As well as unpleasant moments, such as the six hundred lawsuits he received from other inventors claiming to have created the telephone, and although he never lost a single case at that time, Glem experienced in his own essence the unpleasant moments of each litigation.

—It is easier to lay claim to an idea in a courtroom, than to conceive one's own —mused Bell, resenting his predicament as he addressed his intangible companion.

—The lives of great figures are fraught with all manner of obstacles, and it is precisely this tumultuous journey that elevates them to a transcendent plane —opined Glem with profound wisdom and gravitas that bespoke his enlightened state.

On the other hand, the traveler was able to witness with immense pleasure the diverse scientific interests of that eminent discoverer. It was a delight to see him devour the British Encyclopedia, which on several occasions served as inspiration for him to delve into new areas of interest.

Later, while strolling with pleasant deliberation through that thrilling life, Glem felt, with the intensity that his constant state of empathy provided, the joy with which Bell recorded each of his thirty patents, both alone and in partnership with a colleague.

In this way, he also witnessed the moment when the distinguished Volta Prize from the French Academy of Sciences was awarded to him. At that moment, the scientist decided to invest the prize money in the development of the photophone. This invention aimed to transmit sound wirelessly, and during the tests, it managed to transmit sounds and voices, through a beam of light, two hundred meters away. Thus, anticipating a century before, the fiber-optic communication systems.

Likewise, he observed him absorbed with other colleagues, in the realization of the first known sound recording systems, whose work focused on trying to imprint a magnetic field, to then reproduce sounds. But despite everyone's strong feelings of frustration, upon having to abandon the idea due to being unable to construct a viable prototype, the basic principles they proposed would achieve practical applications almost a century later in the tape recorder, hard disk drives, floppy disks, and other magnetic storage media.

In the same vein, the lad shared the anguish experienced by the tireless inventor when, under immense pressure and in a hurry, he developed the first version of a metal detector in an unfortunately failed attempt to extract a bullet lodged in the body of the US President, James Garfield, who had been the victim of an attack that would ultimately prove fatal. Equally, he felt the immense sorrow of the scientist when he determined, sadly too late, how the metal frame of the patient's bed had notably disrupted the functioning of his apparatus.

Furthermore, the youth also witnessed the moment when that distinguished figure, along with other collaborators, founded the National Geographic Society, which emerged as an international organization dedicated to education, science, and geography, and whose monthly magazine "National Geographic" was one of the curious lad's favorite readings.

That captivating and passionate journey culminated as the entity of Glem traveled to the beautiful Beinn Bhreagh peninsula in the province of Nova Scotia, Canada, owned by Graham Bell, to bid him farewell. Despite the devoted care of his beloved wife, the seventy-five-year-old inventor could not escape succumbing to the pernicious anemia that plagued him.

—As I depart, I feel a sense of tranquility. I have always pursued my passions with fervor and savored the company of my loved ones at every turn —spoke the renowned character, bidding farewell to the traveler with heartfelt words.

—It is true, my esteemed professor, and I can assure you that your life and works will be remembered and valued forever. You are one of the greatest examples that significant innovations can indeed be developed through peace, in contrast to those who claim that the most important technological advancements have been products of war —replied the sensitive Glem, as he felt the spirit of Alexander slowly leaving his body and dissipating into space.

EUROPE

In that moment, the traveler felt a comforting peace wash over him, and from that state, he decided to continue his journey towards the meeting of another renowned figure, just as he had previously planned. He called upon the acting techniques he had painstakingly practiced in order to tune into a genuine feeling of originality —the third word on the list— so that he could visit the character he had previously selected.

Once he achieved the appropriate level of concentration, he was pleasantly surprised to find that his actions yielded the desired results. In a mere instant, he was able to transport himself to the place of countless door-lined hallways, and by further intensifying that feeling, he soon found himself standing before a portal which he perceived to be the correct one. Determined and confident, he crossed through it without hesitation.

Suddenly, Glem appeared in a colorful bullring on a beautifully sunny day. The really joyous music and uproar of the crowd served as a backdrop for the celebrated bullfighter's skills.

As soon as Glem brought the character to mind, he found himself standing beside a young boy who was deeply excited, watching every move of the matador with keen interest and shouting «Olé» in unison with the rest of the audience. The child, around eight years old, noticed the presence of the young traveler and turned his gaze toward him, smiling with innocence as if welcoming him. Then, with a small gesture of his head, he indicated that Glem could take a seat in a nearby empty chair next to his family. Immediately, the child turned his attention back to the ring, where a magnificent picador was making his entrance on a gleaming horse. The boy's eyes lit up, shining like two blazing suns. Glem had never before witnessed such a spectacle, and although he defined himself as a conscious defender of nature and animal life, the wonderful emotion that the child transmitted to him somehow made him enjoy the event.

After the dazzling spectacle had concluded, the traveler found himself magically transported to a cherished moment from the childhood of the character before him. With pride swelling in his chest, the young boy approached his father to display a work of art he had created on the lid of a cigar box. The strict painting professor scrutinized the piece with careful consideration, but then, to the boy's great delight, he praised the mastery of composition and color present in the original oil painting.

—This is my first painting, and I never want to part with it —thought the little one, communicating silently with the traveler.

—Every work that we create will always be a part of us, and it is impossible to completely detach ourselves from them —replied the youth, feeling him embraced the sense of contentment emanating from his interlocutor.

In that wondrous moment, Glem beheld the pictorial masterpiece known as "The Yellow Picador," the first creation of the individual who would later be revered as the Mozart of painting, the legendary Pablo Picasso.

For the youth, the pleasure he experienced in accompanying the young Picasso was indescribable. At just thirteen years of age, and without any formal academic training, the budding artist held his first exhibition to great critical acclaim. In each of his works, one could detect the overflowing passion that this character harbored for drawing and painting, —among other artistic disciplines that he would later explore—.

This impulse led to yet another magnificent moment, as the following year, Glem closely followed Picasso's admission process to the school of arts and crafts of "La Lonja" in Barcelona, Spain.

Thanks to his innate skill, the young man was able to gain admission in record time. The level of astonishment was unparalleled when the father of the young artist confessed to his son that he had decided to stop painting and support him in his education, as he felt that his son had already far surpassed him in the artistic realm.

Later, positioning himself in another stage of the artist's life, the traveler witnessed a tragic moment. The news of the suicide of his dear friend Carlos Casagemas plunged Picasso into intense pain and great sadness. This event led to an almost unprecedented occurrence in the world of art. In addition to isolating the characters in his works, which he often placed in ambiguous settings as a reflection of his loneliness, the artist almost exclusively employed the color blue in all of his paintings, extending this peculiar period for more than two years.

Additionally, during that time, Glem was able to appreciate the beauty of early 20th century Paris with immense pleasure. However, he also witnessed the difficult beginnings of Picasso in the French capital. His economic situation was complicated, to say the least. In this sense, the artist sometimes decided to reuse canvases, painting a new work over a previous idea, sometimes completed, simply because he did not have enough money to buy more materials.

Nevertheless, the immense talent of the painter and his astonishing work rhythm —because at that time he could paint one or two paintings per night— soon led to a Parisian art dealer hiring him, paying him 150 francs a month for all the works he produced. In this way, the artist no longer had to visit Laffite Street to try to sell his paintings. At that moment, Glem was not simply overwhelmed by the young painter's happiness at landing his first commission at that time, but also perceived how the first love struck Picasso's heart.

She was a young Parisian of twenty-one years, who worked as a model for artists, and such was her charm, that she was nicknamed the beautiful Fernanda among her peers. Both of them fell deeply in love, as one might expect, and from that moment on, the painter made her his muse. Glem, for his part, was especially pleased with this turn of events, since he always shared the emotional state of the character and had not felt comfortable experiencing the affliction that had previously invaded the artist. Indeed, this event was so positive that from that moment on, all of the painter's friends and acquaintances witnessed a sudden change in his work. He began his pink period, which was characterized primarily by the representation of animals, clowns, and circus characters in his paintings, as well as the paintings he dedicated to his wife. This period was marked by a more joyful and festive tone, reflecting the painter's newfound happiness and inspiration.

Soon, the young traveler found himself at one of the greatest moments in the history of modern art, and this fact confirmed —without a shadow of a doubt— the wisdom of his choice, for this individual was an undisputed representative of the concept of originality. At that time, it was common to see Picasso and his great friend, the French painter Georges Braque, visiting each other's studios to exchange ideas and opinions. Pablo, who was known for his deeply disruptive attitude towards the prevailing classical art of the time, always sought to imbue his works with a life of their own, and he found in his friend the ideal collaborator with whom he created the marvelous artistic movement that would later be baptized —by a renowned French art critic— as "Cubism". And, as if that were not enough, Picasso was also the creator of the collage —as we know it today— being the first artist to introduce it as part of his plastic works. For Glem, it was a delight to feel, through his ethereal body, the pleasure that the artist infected him with every time he put a new and original idea into practice. Sometimes, the boy even perceived as if he himself was the one sticking the fragments of wallpaper or newspaper that ended up complementing the strokes of some paintings.

As the young traveler journeyed onward, he bore witness to a singular moment among many others. It was when the artist presented to the public one of his greatest cubist works, "Les Demoiselles d'Avignon," a portrait intentionally distorted to depict five prostitutes from the popular streets of Barcelona. The opinions among specialized critics and the general public could not have been more divided. Some deemed it grotesque and even absurd, while others defended it as a groundbreaking form of art, both modern and incomparably original. What made this event even more intriguing was the artist's almost complete disregard for the opinions of his critics and detractors, dedicating him entirely to expressing his ideas.

However, Glem soon experienced a sense of regret when the prolific artistic production of his two great friends was unexpectedly truncated with the arrival of the First World War. Georges Braque, co-creator of Cubism, decided to enlist in the French army to fight for his country. Once again, wars appeared in the traveler's frame of experience. As for the Spanish painter, he continued to develop that innovative style on his own.

Furthermore, the young man quickly discovered how tumultuous and eventful the artist's life was. On one occasion, he witnessed the Parisian police interrogating Picasso and a friend of his in relation to the theft of the Mona Lisa from the Louvre museum. Although both were proven innocent, suspicions were aroused because years earlier the painter, through this friend, had acquired certain Iberian primitive art statues without realizing that they had been stolen from the same museum.

Subsequently, the young man felt immense joy in accompanying the tireless figure in another fascinating facet of his life. When he was hired to create the sets and costumes for the Russian ballet during their tour of Europe, he was able to unleash all of his creativity and talent, as always, to the delight of the attending public.

Glem also had the opportunity to witness firsthand how the painter's fame grew relentlessly.

When he was invited to exhibit his works at the Museum of Modern Art in New York, barely a year after its opening, his consecration as a great international artist was unquestionable. In no time, Pablo acquired the first of several castles that he bought during his life. It was immensely pleasurable for that young man to witness how Picasso filled, with his many and varied works, the vast spaces of each of the grandiose buildings that he acquired.

The traveler undoubtedly relished the distinctive personality of the Spaniard, particularly his sharp sense of humor. He found himself in countless situations where he admired the brilliant wit of this character.

On one occasion, Picasso invited a group of friends to his residence. They were taken aback to see that not a single one of his own paintings adorned the walls of his home. When they asked him about it, the man from Malaga quipped, *"The problem is that they're so expensive, I can't afford them"*. At that moment, everyone present burst into laughter in unison due to the artist's wit.

Another amusing incident that Glem witnessed occurred during a flight from Nice to Paris. In the same first-class compartment sat a wealthy American art collector, who recognized the painter and struck up a conversation. The collector asked.

—Please do tell me something, —the collector said—. Why don't you paint people as they really are?

—I fail to comprehend —responded Picasso.

—Well, then why don't you paint people as they are? —persisted the collector—. For instance, when I look at any of your paintings, they just aren't realistic. You put an eye in the middle of the forehead, a nose where the ear should be. It seems utterly ridiculous and entirely wrong. I don't think it's real, and I don't think it's art!

—I still don't understand what you're trying to tell me —the artist replied once again.

—Very well then, let me show you something to make you understand what I mean —the gentleman replied. With that, he took a photograph from his wallet and continued—. Looks; this is my wife, just as she really is.

—Ahh, I understand now —said Picasso in a serious tone—. Your wife is excessively thin and measures about 4 inch.

After that humorous incident, the traveler proceeded to a stunning French beach. Picasso was engrossed in his reading as he sat in a cozy recliner on a bright and sunny morning. He was abruptly interrupted by a young child who begged him for a drawing while holding a piece of paper. The artist soon deduced that the boy had been sent by his parents in an effort to obtain one of his works for free when he grasped the request's nature. The artist immediately threw away the paper after making a few unique strokes and signing his name on the back of the infant. The child ran off happily, while Pablo, mentally addressing Glem, said.

—I wonder. At what moment his parents will allow him to go for a swim?

—Ha! I think after this experience, they'll think twice before trying to take advantage of an artist —the young boy replied, still chuckling at the incident.

After, and as the young man accompanied the painter, they arrived at a joyful lunch where he shared with a group of good friends. When it came time to pay the bill, everyone agreed that Picasso —who by that time was a wealthy artist— should foot the bill. Pablo accepted the proposal without any objection and took out his pen to draw a sketch on a cloth napkin, with the clear intention of using it as payment. However, the proprietor, upon realizing what was happening, spoke to him.

—Could you please sign it for me? —the lady was visibly excited.

—Forgive me, my lady, but I intend to pay for the lunch, not to buy the whole restaurant.

Having witnessed so many moments charged with sharp wit, Glem unexpectedly found himself transported to the moment of the creation of the painter's masterpiece. To contemplate the entire process of imagination, conception, and development of the painting that, like few others, served to immortalize the great Pablo Picasso, was an experience completely indescribable. At that time, the General Director of Fine Arts in Spain commissioned the artist to create a work to be exhibited in the Spanish pavilion during an international exposition to be held in Paris. As the objective was to attract international attention to the Republican cause during the Spanish Civil War, Picasso began sketching what now the famous painting is called "Guernica." A monumental mural measuring 11.45 feet tall by 25.5 feet wide, this refers to the infamous bombing of the civilian population of that Basque town by the German and Italian air forces in support of the rebel faction during the Spanish Civil War.

The young man, with almost the sensitivity of an art critic, was able to appreciate the immense artistic value of that masterpiece, by interpreting the extraordinary symbolism with which the author sought to express the suffering that war inflicts on human beings.

Even the traveler was also a spectator of a very particular encounter related to this prominent work.

On one occasion, the ambassador of Nazi Germany in France, who was a passionate art collector, visited the painter in his Parisian studio when he was finishing the mural. Upon appreciating the marvelous painting, he courteously addressed the artist, saying.

—I think this is the best thing you've ever done!

—Excuse me, but I haven't done this, you have! —Pablo responded with brilliance, he referred openly to the German responsibility for the bombing.

The fact was that Picasso's distinctive and strong personality inevitably permeated every sphere he touched. In this regard, the traveler observed how, although Pablo had joined the French Communist Party, he not only did not follow the strict guidelines that this political organization tried to impose on its members, but he also openly criticized whenever he felt something was not right. Equally, Glem witnessed the great humanity of this character, as he helped many Spanish republicans exiled in France, yet these acts were never publicized, as Picasso always assumed these actions with genuine honesty and privacy.

Leaving aside the moments of sublime creation of his works, as well as the amusing anecdotes in the life of the artist, Glem suddenly found himself traversing the tumultuous love affair of the artist.

He discovered how Picasso's relationship with the women in his life was very complicated —to put it simply—. The painter was married twice, but also had several mistresses, whom he sometimes did not hide from his wife. As a result of these complex romantic relationships, he had four children with three different women.

The traveler himself could sense how the painter felt a profound attraction to women; they were his muses, his impulse, and the object of his most unrestrained desires. Thus, he witnessed how during his life, he was stringing along lovers, for he had not ended one relationship when he already began another. These situations —without any deliberate intention— left deep traces of pain on his companions, some of whom ended their lives in very unfortunate circumstances.

As Glem traversed this particular passage in the life of the illustrious character, he inevitably found himself at the end of his journey. The young man was present in the imposing mansion of Mougins in France, the property of the painter, observing how at ninety-one years of age, and due to a pulmonary edema, the artist left his physical body behind, leaving an immeasurable artistic legacy behind.

—I lived fully and in my own way, that's why I don't regret anything —were Pablo's final words addressed to the young traveler.

—Your life, my admired genius, is the greatest example of personal achievement through contemporary art. I feel that I have learned so much, especially from your great authenticity. Thank you for your invaluable legacy! —Glem's response was clearly moved by the recent experience.

Thus, another fantastic adventure of the passionate traveler came to an end.

Once he returned to his senses and was out of the pyramid, Glem hurried to find pencil and paper to copy the important piece of information he had observed during his encounter with Graham Bell. With total confidence, he wrote down the number 1874072611, which corresponded to the serial assigned by the inventor to one of his telephonic devices.

At that precise moment, the young boy noticed the wall clock, and his surprise was overwhelming as he realized that it was 1:11 AM —the same time at which his first journey had ended—. This made him reflect on the complex factors associated with the nature of those travels, which completely escaped his control and understanding.

VERIFICATION

In the days following his last journey, Glem was immersed in the design of an elaborate plan that would allow him to discern whether those travels were real or simply the product of his prodigious imagination. He spent hours researching how to achieve an aging effect on paper that would be truly believable. In fact, to obtain the ideal raw material with which he would create the document he wanted to forge, he had to travel to another province, so he requested a two-day permit from his job. Then, when he considered that he had achieved a good result, he set out to capture —relying on his memory— a blueprint showing the different faces of that prototype telephone whose serial number he had memorized.

After completing this first part of the process, he dedicated himself to conducting a thorough investigation about the Bell farm, which currently operates as one of the museums dedicated to the inventor, and in whose workshop he remembers having been several times during his journey. Glem was determined to pay a visit, but as he had considered before, he decided to seek company for the trip.

Thus, Glem met with his two coworkers, Sandra and Marcos. He told them that the mysterious book he had been reading gave him some clues to obtain an unknown blueprint that apparently belonged to Alexander Graham Bell. His surprise was enormous when, in the days he was absent from the library, following the coordinates of the text, he managed to find the enigmatic document. At that moment, he proposed that they accompany him to visit the famous Melville House —named after Alexander Graham's father— located in southern Ontario. According to the book, they could verify the legitimacy of that ancient drawing there.

As expected, his two friends were visibly excited and imbued with that daring spirit that characterizes youth, and they accepted the proposal immediately. As soon as Glem informed them that he had already found their respective replacements during the time of the trip, as well as having booked train tickets and accommodation in Toronto, they began to jump with excitement, like children.

—Thank you for once again embodying the adventurous spirit that has always defined you, my dear friend —Sandra uttered, addressing the trip's organizer.

—I haven't ceased to be myself, maybe I was just busy with other things —the young man replied, sporting a self-satisfied smile.

The day of their journey arrived swiftly, and with great enthusiasm, the three young people departed from the Ottawa train terminal bound for Toronto's Union Station. They planned to spend the night in the city before departing the next day for the small town of Brantford, home to the Bell farm.

During the roughly five-hour train ride, Glem regaled his companions with fascinating facts about the inventor's life. They were clearly amazed, as well as excited; by the level of detail their friend was able to convey, not to mention his marvelous storytelling ability.

—Let's see dear friends, does anyone know who was the inventor of the telephone? —asked Glem.

—I've always believed it to be Alexander Graham Bell, but by the way you're asking, I suspect you're about to surprise us —replied Marcos, intrigued.

—I shall begin by saying that if you were on a TV game show, you would have been eliminated at this very moment —the young man commented, flashing a sly smile—. Allow me to tell you the whole story. In 1854, the Italian Antonio Meucci constructed a prototype of the telephone, which he called the "Teletrophone." However, he did not have enough money to patent it at the time, so he continued to refine his design. In 1871, he presented the description of his invention at the United States Patent Office. Five years later, Bell formally patented his own telephone design and established the company that marketed it. For many years, Alexander Graham Bell was considered the inventor of the telephone, but doubts about his authorship arose when it was discovered that he had access to Meucci's documents, which were housed in the Patent Office. For this reason, this year, the United States Congress, after decades of discussion, passed a resolution recognizing the Italian as the true inventor of the telephone.

—I've always admired your ability to turn history into a narrative about relatable people. Please tell me you have more tales like that. It'll make the journey seem shorter —Sandra commented, clearly excited.

—Well, let it be known that you're asking for it —Glem exclaimed in a playful tone, as his companions laughed and settled into their seats—. Bell's contribution to the development of the telephone was so significant that it overshadowed other equally innovative and important inventions. This great figure, both alone and in collaboration, created various devices, including the phonograph, some airborne vehicles like the hydroplane, a steel lung that aided in artificial respiration, an audiometer to detect mild hearing problems, an intriguing device for locating icebergs, as well as research on how to separate salt from seawater and even work that anticipated the search for alternative fuels.

The enthusiastic young man continued to share his friends with a series of anecdotes and little-known details about the inventor's life, which made their long journey particularly enjoyable. Finally, they arrived in Toronto and retired to their hotel to rest, as they planned to visit the Bell museum the following day.

The next morning, as they had agreed, the three friends met for breakfast. Glem informed them that they planned to leave for their destination around noon, suggesting that they take a stroll around the city before departing. They all agreed that it was an excellent idea.

And so, they embarked on a delightful tour of the beautiful downtown of cosmopolitan Toronto. The three young people were captivated, marveling at how the modern skyscrapers contrasted with the variety buildings of classical architecture in the area. The wide avenues, elegant restaurants, beautiful boulevard along Lake Ontario, and the iconic 1,814-feet CN tower made the journey an extremely enjoyable one.

During their stroll, they stumbled upon the renowned Art Gallery of Ontario, one of North America's largest art museums. To Glem's surprise, there was an announcement at the entrance inviting visitors to appreciate a recent installation of works by none other than the great painter, Pablo Picasso.

This fortuitous event prompted him to consider visiting the exhibition. However, he knew they wouldn't have time to do so that same day, so he proposed the idea to the group and they agreed to visit the place early the next day before returning to Ottawa.

When it was time to depart, they boarded the train once again, which would take them to Brantford in just two hours. Upon arrival, they found themselves standing before a beautiful country house with an ivory-colored facade. The wooden columns of the front porch painted white and delicately carved with diamond-shaped figures, along with its long windows and refined door, revealed the extraordinary preservation work that had been done to maintain the place.

As soon as they began their journey, they were amazed to see how every space remained identical to when the Bell family resided on the property. With only fifteen minutes left until the place closed, the trio arrived at a parlor where a collection of artifacts lay. Immediately, Glem recognized the rudimentary telephone device for which they had made the journey.

—What would you like to know? —asked a friendly and charming young woman, who worked as a guide of the place.

—We are employees of the Parliamentary Library in Ottawa, and we have brought a document that we would like to compare with one of the devices resting in this room —Glem replied, showing the young guide his work credentials and a letter allegedly from the Library's management addressed to the museum.

—Oh, how intriguing! —exclaimed the young guide—. Please allow me to call my supervisor to attend to you.

—Certainly, Wendy! —said the young man, having read the name on the small badge affixed to her uniform—. Before you go, may I show you the document we have brought and explain what we wish to compare? Our aim is to verify its authenticity —with confidence, he hastened to display the blueprint he had crafted, specifically pointing out the serial number he wished to examine.

—I understand. I see that you wish to examine Mr. Bell's first telephone apparatus.

—Exactly so! —exclaimed the cunning young man, hoping to sway the girl's decision—. That is why we would like you to allow us to cross the security line, in your presence, of course. Time is of the essence, as we have a long journey ahead and our transportation awaits us.

—I sense an unusual urgency in your request —replied the guide with a hint of suspicion—. Let us do this instead: allow me to review that blueprint once again.

Glem promptly handed over the drawing, and as the guide examined it more closely, she addressed the visitors.

—It seems that there is no need for me to contact my superior, nor will we have to enter the room —declared the confident young guide, after scrutinizing the drawing—. Although this blueprint is very well crafted, it is in fact a forgery. Just like all of Mr. Bell's plans, it was dimensioned using the English system of units. However, toward the end of his career and after his passing, his team of collaborators added annotations in the International System of Units to all his documents. As you can see, this blueprint lacks those two annotations.

At that moment, Glem was speechless, for the brilliant young woman was undoubtedly right. He had followed the inventor's trajectory and works closely during his journey but had not paid much attention to the work of Bell's assistants and associates. However, just as he thought the entire mission had failed, his good friend Marcos came to the rescue.

—We do not doubt everything you have told us —Marcos took the floor and spoke to the young woman—. However if I manage to guess correctly in three matters, would you help us verify the information we came to seek?

—Let me hear it then —the young woman replied, her curiosity piqued.

—Firstly, I must say that you are undoubtedly a Latina, and I dare say, from Mexico —said the young man, exhibiting an extraordinary talent for identifying accents.

—In that, you have guessed correctly, but it is not difficult to discern, for my accent and my Latin features are evident, and furthermore, our community is one of the largest in Canada —the young woman replied, not feeling surprised at all—. But why do you say that? Are we fellow countrymen?

—No, I am from Colombia, but I have dear Mexican friends, and I agree with you, they are a joyous and vast community. Now then, I shall continue. I also believe that you graduated with an engineering degree from your country, and specialized in the field of mechanics.

—Wow! I confess that I did not see that coming. I don't know how you did it, but you hit the nail on the head in both cases —replied the guide, notably astonished.

—Rest easy, do not be alarmed. I am merely an astute observer. I noticed the beautiful graduation ring you wear, and from the color of the gemstone, I knew you were an engineer. Furthermore, your adept handling of measurement systems terminology led me to presume your area of expertise —replied the young man, reassuringly.

—I understand now, everything seems to make more sense —replied the young woman with a tone of relief.

—And lastly, I dare to affirm that this museum doesn't maintain a continuous and mandatory policy of exchanging pieces, documents, or information with other sites that may contain the inventor's pieces, correct? —said Marcos, with a hint of astuteness in his expression.

—Indeed it is! But what is your point? —asked the perplexed young woman.

—Allow me to explain. I'm trying to say that there is a possibility that Bell, for some personal reason, may have kept a document in his private archives that refers to his greatest invention, and that this document may not have passed through the hands of his assistants and you may not be aware of it.

—Yes, that's probable —the young woman replied.

—Then, I propose something to you. You could enter the room alone, take the device, look at the back of the base, and with me facing away, I will dictate the serial to you. That way, we will all be sure.

—I think you have convinced me. Alright, let's give it a try —replied the girl with a sense of determination.

The young woman entered the room, picked up the artifact, and before Marcos could even speak, she expressed her difficulty in distinguishing the numbers on it due to the wooden base being riddled with marks. Glem, however, had already anticipated this possibility and quickly offered her a small piece of white chalk, suggesting that she gently rub it over the numbers to make them more visible. She did so and as soon as she could identify the digits, she announced that she was ready. Marcos began reciting the serial number, and to the surprise of everyone present, each of the ten digits matched perfectly.

At that moment, Glem's level of excitement was truly indescribable. Thanks to the strategic selection of that great character, he had been able to verify the truth of time travel.

After the peculiar meeting had ended, the closing time of the venue had arrived, and all those present bid each other farewell in a cordial manner. As for the shrewd Marcos, he managed to exchange contact information with the charming Wendy. It was evident that he had been captivated by the beauty and intelligence of that young woman.

On their way back to Toronto, the three friends laughed, reminiscing about how they had managed to solve that intricate situation.

Then, Glem suddenly changed the subject and asked his companions what they thought if he told them some stories about Picasso, since they had decided to visit the exhibition the next day. Almost instinctively, his companions responded with a resounding yes.

And so, the excited traveler began to chronologically recount the story of the painter, starting from his early beginnings, passing through the various stages he experienced, his masterpieces, the immense contributions he made to modern visual arts, as well as his tempestuous romantic relationships. And towards the end of his engaging narration, he remarked.

—As you may have noticed, he was a character far ahead of his time —spoke the young man as if he were giving an art history class—. But something that many may not know is that this great painter, in addition to being a sculptor, ceramicist, and set designer, was also a poet and playwright. What's interesting is that he took this facet very seriously, as he managed to write three hundred poems and two plays. He even once said that perhaps after his death, he would be remembered as *"Pablo Ruiz Picasso: Spanish poet and playwright. He also happened to paint a few pictures"* —immediately, all present burst into laughter at such a witty anecdote—. But beyond all that I have told you —he said—, there is something that, in honor of his undisputed greatness, I consider must be especially highlighted, and I'm referring to his tireless work capacity. Pablo created art throughout his life and practically uninterrupted. He always carried his work tools with him, even when he took what he considered to be vacations. In fact, he had several workshops at the same time, located in different properties.

The result of this incredible work pace allowed him, during his seventy-five-year career, to create a titanic body of work composed of thirteen thousand five hundred paintings and designs, around one hundred thousand prints and engravings, thirty-four thousand book illustrations, and three hundred sculptures and pieces of ceramics. He is the only artist capable of exhibiting such a prolific body of work, and it is also why his works have been the most stolen in history —this is how the young man finished his pleasant presentation, at the same time that the train arrived at the last station.

The next day, the three friends arrived a few minutes before the museum opening time. Knowing they had to leave in a couple of hours to head back home, they headed straight to the section of the museum where the painter's exhibition was located. They were all marveling at the variety of the artist's paintings while the young traveler occasionally pointed out to his companions which period each painting belonged to.

Suddenly, Glem was paralyzed at the sight of a particular painting. It was "The Blue Room" a beautiful and simple painting that depicted a stylized woman taking a bath in front of her bed, in a very modest room. His friends, noticing his strange reaction, asked him what was happening, and why that painting, with its simple strokes compared to the more elaborate pieces, was causing him such emotion. The young man replied.

—In my understanding, this work belongs to a young Picasso, who had recently moved to Paris in search of fortune. Due to the economic precarity of his beginnings, he would sometimes reuse his canvases, even after having already made a painting on them. That is why I believe there is another painting behind the one we see, and I would even venture to say that it is a portrait of a bearded man —concluded Glem, speaking with the confidence of one who had witnessed the event firsthand.

Unbeknownst to the young man, his entire explanation had been overheard by one of the museum's curator, who was not only in charge of the exhibition, but also an expert on the artist's work. Thus, the lady approached the traveler, somewhat intrigued.

—Excuse me, young man. I couldn't help but overhear your words —so the museum employee started a conversation—. I am surprised by the accuracy of your description. I wonder if you belong to the research team of the Phillips Collection, since it is evident that you have accurate and privileged information about the artwork. Please accept my apologies in advance if my question makes you uncomfortable.

—Don't worry, you haven't bothered me in the slightest —the young man replied politely—. I must say that I'm not part of the group you mentioned, and as for how I have this knowledge, it's because I work for the Library of Parliament in Ottawa and my aunt is the Minister of Canadian Culture and Heritage. By chance, I came across an article that referenced this case, and I found it so interesting that it stuck in my memory.

—Now I understand perfectly, thank you for the clarification and I invite you to continue enjoying the tour —said the kind lady as she bid them farewell and headed off to attend to other matters.

The trio, as they glanced at the time, realized it was time to head to the train station. They did so and once the journey had commenced, Sandra posed a question to her best friend.

—Glem, tell us, how did you know about the hidden painting? And why did you make up that story about your aunt and the library? —she demanded eager to uncover the truth.

—My dear friends, I think it's time for you to know the truth —the young man took a deep breath, preparing himself to reveal his secret—. The mysterious book that has kept me so absorbed is a kind of manual for building a machine and traveling through time. I followed all the steps indicated, and not only did I manage to travel, but this journey we just took together proved to me that these peculiar expeditions are real.

The two young people could hardly believe what they had just heard, but before they could even ask a question, Glem began to recount all the events he had experienced since starting his time travel journey. The return trip was undoubtedly even more entertaining than the previous transfers, as the traveler recounted all his experiences in detail —as was his style—, from the moment of his preparation, the construction of the quantum machine, his first and second trips, the planning of the Bell farm adventure, and how fate led him

—seemingly unexpectedly—, to the encounter with Picasso's painting.

Upon arriving at their final destination, the two friends thanked Glem for inviting them to live such an exciting adventure and for trusting them by confessing his incredible secret. For his part, the young man expressed that it was he who should thank them for accompanying him on that crazy excursion and that he now felt better for having shared his unusual story.

Once the young traveler found himself alone in his room, he reflected deeply on everything he had experienced during those three days. Thus, maintaining his state of total openness, he knew he had to trust the flow of events, while repeating to him mentally, «Everything is fine, everything is perfect».

From that moment on, he experienced with special emotion the passing of time, to carry out his third and final journey.

CHAPTER IV

THE THIRD JOURNEY

"Hate is a feeling that is as base as it is useless,
since it consumes the person who harbors it
without affecting the object of their emotion"

Just a few days before embarking on his third and final journey, Glem once again experienced, albeit to a lesser extent, the emotional inertia that always followed each expedition. Aware that this sensation might intensify after his upcoming adventure, he began to consider possible alternatives to cope with this situation. After one of his meditation sessions, an idea came to his mind, and he decided to contact his aunt Lena once again, seeking her support.

One day he called the minister, and in her office, they informed him that she was currently representing Canada at a major international conference in the Netherlands and would not be back for another week. They assured him that they would pass on the message to the minister about his call. The young man thanked them for the information and bid them a polite farewell.

A couple of days later, Glem was pleasantly surprised by an eagerly awaited communication. The renowned University of Ottawa informed him that his application to the Honours bachelor's in "International Development and Globalization" had been accepted.

Overwhelmed with excitement, he thought about running to tell his mother, but he paused for a moment and decided to do something even better. Determined to surprise her, he set out to prepare a special dinner. His mother had taught him how to cook, and he was quite skilled at it, so he got to work and crafted a sumptuous menu. It consisted of a flavorful hibachi-style salad with a Filipino-style sweet and sour dressing as the appetizer, a delicious salmon risotto accompanied by fresh asparagus and exquisitely seasoned vegetables as the main course, and a carefully selected Chardonnay white wine with tropical fruit notes for the perfect pairing. For dessert, he chose canned peach slices in syrup with a cream cheese topping.

As Ada arrived home, caught off guard, she was pleasantly surprised. The table was beautifully set with all the dishes delicately arranged, and at the base of an elegant candelabrum adorned with flickering candles, lay an envelope containing a letter with the wonderful news.

—Oh, my child! What a splendid surprise. Do tell me what we are celebrating.

—Go ahead and see for yourself —replied Glem as he handed her the envelope.

—My beloved son! What wonderful news —exclaimed his mother, tears welling up in her eyes as she embraced her son with immense pride—. Your father would be so proud of you right now.

—I know he is, Mother. Wherever his essence may be, he is aware of my achievements and takes pride in my successes —replied the young man wisely, now understanding the concept of dimensions that surround us in a different light.

Both enjoyed that dinner to the fullest, conversing and reminiscing beautiful moments from the past. Ada felt a mix of excitement and tranquility, knowing well the maturity of her son and the soundness of his decisions. Moreover, it was always a great relief to know that the financial aspect was taken care of, thanks to the foresight of Glem Smith, who had acquired a generous trust fund plan to cover his son's tuition fees, which would be released when he turned twenty-one, a situation that was soon to happen.

And so, when the day came for Glem to embark on his last scheduled expedition through time, he experienced mixed feelings. While he had relished every adventure to the fullest, he knew that once he started his university studies, it would be challenging to maintain the rigorous regimen of comprehensive conditioning required for each journey. Nevertheless, he decided to set aside those thoughts and allow himself to flow with the events.

As Glem began the customary ritual and smoothly located the door that seemed to beckon to him the most, he crossed its threshold only to find himself confronted with a situation utterly unforeseen.

As Glem stood in front of a grand two-story house, he witnessed a shocking scene unfolding before his eyes. A young boy, no older than twelve, leaped from a second-story window and plummeted to the ground. The boy landed feeling pain, and upon noticing Glem's presence, he immediately addressed him with a question:

—Who are you? Am I dead?

—You can rest assured! You haven't died. I am a good friend, only you are capable of perceiving —replied Glem, with a reassuring tone.

Immediately after, the young boy fainted, while the traveler, due to his usual connection, could feel a certain degree of pain in his ethereal body.

After a brief moment, the traveler understood the cause of what had happened. The young boy, who by that time was already conscious in a hospital room, had attempted to take his own life because he felt guilty for the death of his grandmother. The thing was, a few days earlier, his parents had left him in the care of his younger brother. However, he had chosen to attend a local parade, and in his absence, the six-year-old boy had fallen down the stairs, causing his grandmother to be startled and suffer a heart attack.

The Traveler, standing by the side of this new character, then found himself in a moment of his life when he was in his first year of sociology at university, only to learn that he had failed his public speaking class. This event compelled young Martin Luther King Jr. to make a commendable effort to develop the powerful oratorical style that he exhibited throughout his tumultuous public life.

It was during the tumultuous times of racial segregation in the United States, when people of color all had stories to tell, and Martin was no exception. One time, when he was just seven years old, two white friends unexpectedly told him that they were no longer allowed to play with him, a situation that deeply marked him. At such a young age, he couldn't comprehend how something as pure as friendship could be dependent on the color of one's skin. Later, in high school, he began dating a German girl who worked as a waitress. Although the feelings were mutual, their romance came to a drastic end when the girl's parents found out that their daughter was dating an African American.

Glem, on the other hand, thoroughly enjoyed every step of the brilliant young man's academic journey. King was so talented that he skipped the ninth and twelfth grades in high school, graduated with a degree in sociology at the age of nineteen, and immediately enrolled to pursue a bachelor's degree in theology. He continued his studies relentlessly until he obtained a doctorate in philosophy at the early age of twenty-six.

That same year, the Traveler witnessed one of the most significant actions led by the already-revered Baptist minister, Martin Luther King Jr. It was when Rosa Parks, a black woman, was arrested for violating segregation laws in the city of Montgomery, Alabama by refusing to give up her seat to a white man on a bus. King initiated a bus boycott, organizing a system of shared rides. The black population supported him and sustained the protest for three hundred and eighty-two days. The reverend himself was arrested during this campaign, and white segregationist groups resorted to terrorist methods to intimidate the black population, even attacking Martin Luther King Jr.'s home with firebombs. But in the end, the boycott ended thanks to a decision by the United States Supreme Court, which declared segregation on buses, restaurants, schools, and other public places in that city illegal. This was one of the first victories that this leader achieved in support of his cause.

The following year, Glem accompanied the character in the founding of the Southern Christian Leadership Conference, a pacifist organization through which he would coordinate several African American churches in various nonviolent protests for civil rights. King, from the beginning of his struggle, decided to embrace the philosophy of nonviolent civil disobedience that Gandhi had successfully implemented in India years before. In this way, his organization strategically chose the locations and methods of protest, repeatedly achieving significant results. Throughout the process, Martin's fame as a great leader and orator continued to rise.

The traveler remembers with particular fondness a poignant moment when Martin Luther King Jr., after concluding an important conference on civil rights, noticed a young black child sitting in the front row, gazing in awe at a multitude of balloons released as part of the event's finale. King picked up the child so that he could get a better view of the spectacle, when suddenly the little one asked him:

—Do the black balloons also fly to the sky?

—The balloons do not fly to the sky based on their color, but on what they carry inside —came the wise response from the illustrious figure.

On the other hand, there were many moments that Glem shared with the King family. However, some of the most cherished ones were the frequent gatherings of all the household members in front of the television, enjoying the popular series Star Trek. Martin always praised the show's progressive themes of racial and social equality, as they aligned with his own ideals. He even took the time to write to the creator of the series, acknowledging the value of its positive message.

One time, when the actress of color who portrayed Lieutenant Uhura in the renowned science fiction show expressed her intention to leave the series after the first season due to feeling that her character lacked depth, the reverend ran into her during a convention. He expressed his admiration for the show and especially for her character, urging her to reconsider her decision. He emphasized that she was a role model for the African American community and that her performance was crucial in representing racial diversity on American television. The actress listened to that advice, and managed to transform her role into one of the key interpretations of that production, thus becoming a benchmark for the society she represented.

Another intriguing event witnessed by the traveler was when the King couple generously offered to pay the hospital bill for a close friend who had just welcomed a beautiful baby girl into the world, but was facing financial difficulties. The proud parents were white Americans, and the wife was a theater school director. It turned out that some time ago, Coretta Scott King —the wife of the Reverend—, had inquired about enrolling her children in the school, and without hesitation, the director had responded positively. In fact, Martin's eldest daughter even had a leading role in a play where she had to kiss a white boy on stage. Despite aggressive reactions from members of the Ku Klux Klan, who had even set a car on fire outside the theater, this did not intimidate them, and the King children continued to attend their classes. This fostered a deep friendship between the two families. The remarkable twist in this story was the discovery that the newborn baby girl was none other than Glem's favorite actress, the beautiful and popular Julia Roberts.

Additionally, one of the moments that Glem enjoyed the most was being present as this great thinker wrote his books, which ultimately became five texts of profound influence for the future. It was particularly his third work, titled "Strength to Love," that deeply moved the traveler. It was an extraordinary collection of sermons and reflections on the struggle for civil rights and the philosophy of nonviolence. The author's impeccable description of what he defined as the spiral of violence struck a chord with the young man, as he could fully identify with the sentiments expressed by this great leader.

"The ultimate weakness of violence is that it is a descending spiral, begetting the very thing it seeks to destroy. Instead of diminishing evil, it multiplies it. Through violence you may murder the liar, but you cannot murder the lie, nor establish the truth. Through violence you may murder the hater, but you do not murder hate. In fact, violence merely increases hate. So it goes... Returning violence for violence multiplies violence, adding deeper darkness to a night already devoid of stars. Darkness cannot drive out darkness: only light can do that. Hate cannot drive out hate: only love can do that."

As Glem embarked on this unique journey, he could hardly believe all the acts of violence he witnessed. While accompanying this great figure in his many campaigns for social justice, he was constantly experiencing, albeit subtly through his ethereal body, a range of emotions such as uncertainty, frustration, sadness, pain, and yet, paradoxically, hope. All of this was the result of the collective energy he perceived from the intense groups of activists with whom Martin Luther King Jr. collaborated.

The traveler, filled with admiration, learned about all the ideals championed by the political activist. He organized and led marches for African Americans' right to vote, desegregation, the right to work, and other basic human rights. The young traveler was particularly struck by the way the leader succinctly summarized his thoughts and actions, as evident during a conference where he declared: *"Cowardice asks the question: Is it safe?*

Expediency asks the question: Is it political? Vanity asks the question: Is it popular? But conscience asks the question: Is it right? And there comes a time when one must take a position that is neither safe, nor political, nor popular. But one must take it because it is right."

On the other hand, King foresaw with great clarity that nonviolent organized protests would garner extensive media coverage of the struggles against segregation. As a result, newspaper articles and television channels began to depict the daily mistreatment and humiliation endured by African Americans in the southern United States, as well as the violence and harassment inflicted by segregationist groups upon civil rights activists. This led to a growing sympathy within society for these movements, which would eventually culminate —albeit regrettably after many years of suffering—, in the enactment of several egalitarian laws.

In none of his previous journeys had the traveler experienced so many moments of shock and anguish. It was during an event where the leader was conducting a book signing in a store in Harlem, New York, that a mentally unbalanced black woman suddenly stabbed the reverend in the chest, accusing him of being a communist. In that moment, Glem himself felt as though he had been wounded. Fortunately, the attack was not fatal, although the letter opener used by the assailant had grazed his aorta. King was promptly rushed to the hospital, where he underwent surgery and began his recovery within days. After recovering from his convalescence, he went to visit his assailant and forgave her.

—People always believe they are doing what's right based on their beliefs and justifications. I am not one to judge, but what is within my control is forgiveness —Martin addressed the traveler in his mind.

—You, unlike many, have always led by example. How much the world leaders could benefit from learning this valuable rule of life —was the young man's response, in a reflective tone.

During the journey, Glem reflected on the challenging moments when certain anti-segregationist groups struggled to achieve tangible results despite strictly adhering to the principles of nonviolent resistance championed by Martin Luther King Jr., however, even when protesters grew visibly frustrated with prolonged battles that seemed futile —such as in Albany, Georgia—, and resorted to violent means, the reverend asserted his authority by demanding an end to the protests and even calling for days of penance.

Nevertheless, the statesmanlike demeanor of this great figure allowed him to learn from mistakes, conducting a thorough self-assessment of past events. He came to the realization that on several occasions, the weakness in their strategies lay in focusing on protesting against segregation in general, rather than concentrating on more specific aspects. In this way, it would have been easier to achieve some form of victory, which would undoubtedly have boosted the morale of all those involved.

With this valuable lesson, the young man witnessed how the leader decided to focus his efforts on the population of Birmingham, Alabama, where the highest degree of racial segregation in the entire country was evident through a local law. The initial strategy proposed was a boycott of the stores and businesses in the area, but the businessmen resisted the protest. At that moment, the reverend put into action a new plan, which consisted of a series of nonviolent demonstrations, such as sit-ins at restaurants and libraries, kneeling in white-only churches, and accompanying all these actions with peaceful marches. The goal was to create a situation of widespread crisis that would foster negotiation between the parties, regardless of how many arrests occurred. It was during these manoeuvers that King himself was arrested, and from there he wrote the famous "Letter from Birmingham Jail," which constitutes a magnificent essay where he clearly outlines his struggle against segregation and passionately declares his crusade for justice and life. However, his time in confinement was brief, thanks to the intervention of President Kennedy himself.

On the other hand, during the actions carried out in this city, the traveler continued to witness brutal scenes of police violence. However, the extensive media coverage provoked an unexpected international reaction, with several analysts comparing these events to the criticized apartheid policy in South Africa. This conflict concluded with a notable victory for the protesters, as the mayor of the city resigned and the police chief was replaced, leading to the removal of segregation signs and the opening of public places for black people.

Then, Glem found himself in another significant episode of history. The preparations for the famous "March on Washington" were fraught with tension and internal conflicts. The government demanded that the speech to be delivered be conciliatory in tone. On the other hand, radical members of the fighting associations believed that complying with that order would mean losing a valuable opportunity.

The long-awaited day arrived, and nearly two hundred and fifty thousand people gathered at the place. The energy radiating from the crowd was indescribable. The young man stood beside the speaker, who, lost in prayer, awaited his turn to address the audience. At that moment, the traveler could sense a strange feeling of restless calm emanating from the figure.

When King took the floor, he began his speech as he had prepared it with his team of advisors. But suddenly, from among the audience, a familiar voice shouted, *"Tell them about your dream"* in clear reference to a sermon the reverend had delivered days earlier. From that moment on, he set aside the papers where his speech was written and, as if he had tapped into divine wisdom, he continued speaking spontaneously. In this way, in a very emotional moment during the conference, he uttered those words that would go down in history, *"I have a dream that my four little children will one day live in a nation where they will not be judged by the color of their skin, but by the content of their character."*

That iconic speech, like never before, invited humanity to be aware of the historic moment they were living in, calling for action and unity in order to achieve a more just and egalitarian society together. He placed special emphasis on the primacy of human dignity and respect above all else. In this way, when the march concluded peacefully, both the government and his fellow activists recognized the significant success achieved.

After one year had passed since that great event, the traveler's emotion was immense when Martin Luther King Jr. became the youngest person ever to be awarded the Nobel Peace Prize for leading a nonviolent resistance campaign aimed at eliminating racial prejudice in the United States.

Not long after, another armed conflict presented itself in the traveler's experience. The Vietnam War caused divided opinions among those who supported the United States' involvement in the conflict and those who were against it. As expected, the reverend vehemently rejected this military intervention. He pointed out that through this reprehensible action, his nation would be treating the Asian country as if it were a colony. Thus, after delivering his powerful speech "Beyond Vietnam: A Time to Break Silence" in New York, and mentioning that the United States was the greatest purveyor of violence in those tumultuous times, several media outlets and political elites harshly criticized him. However, this great leader remained steadfast, supported by his ideals.

—The war is the most palpable evidence of man's estrangement from God and his infinite love, it has been so, it is so, and it will be so. However, there are many who attack me, saying that I am the one who is mistaken —commented the reverend, addressing Glem.

—Time will prove you are right, and those who oppose you today will acknowledge the greatness of yours thoughts tomorrow —replied the young person with immense confidence.

After these tumultuous moments, Glem found himself present at a particular sermon by the reverend, delivered in Memphis, Tennessee. In it, the figure made reference to how God had allowed him to climb the mountain and from there; he could see the Promised Land. He expressed that he might not accompany them, but he was happy to know that his people would eventually reach their destination. He stated that, like anyone else, he would desire a long life, but he was not worried about that matter and he did not fear the threats made against him. He simply wished to fulfill God's will. That prophetic talk ended with applause from an ecstatic audience.

The next day, the young man accompanied the leader along with several friends and colleagues in a hotel room, all waiting for the time to attend an important celebration. Suddenly, the reverend went out to the balcony to get some fresh air, and instantly a gunshot was heard. Martin Luther King Jr. fell to the ground with a bullet wound in his neck, inflicted by a sniper. Upon hearing the noise, everyone present rushed to his aid. During that chaotic moment, Glem perceived the gravity of the event as he felt the magnitude of the wound in his own astral body. In that instant, while the leader was agonizing, his last words were directed to his dear friend, the flutist Ben Branch, who was the leader of the band scheduled to perform at the event. *"Ben, be ready to play "Precious Lord, Take My Hand" at the meeting tonight. Play it in the most beautiful way."*

One hour later, that great leader had departed, despite the efforts of several doctors at a city hospital. Glem lived with anguish and sorrow every minute of that fateful moment. However, his surprise was immense, as unlike all his previous journeys, the journey did not end with the physical departure of that person. For the spirit of the reverend remained by his side, and in this way, they both moved at the speed of their synchronized thoughts, witnessing the events that unfolded after the assassination. Thus, as requested by the leader himself, his widow made arrangements for his funeral oration to be the last sermon recorded by himself at the Ebenezer Baptist Church in Atlanta, Georgia, where he had been a reverend until the end of his days. In his words, he requested that his awards not be mentioned, but instead, it should be mentioned that he had tried to feed the hungry, clothe the naked, plead for an end to war, and that he had loved and served humanity at all times. It was a deeply moving moment, and both the presence of King and the traveler were imbued with the energy and profound emotions that embraced the more than three hundred thousand people who attended the funeral, including the Vice President of the United States himself.

The unique meeting of the two intangible beings continued, and both witnessed with sorrow the riots that erupted in over a hundred cities, prompting the government to deploy the military forces to the streets in order to gain control of the situation. Particularly in the capital of the country, the violence from the Afro Descendant community was much more intense than in other places.

—I feel sorrow for what is happening, I never wished for my departure to provoke these kinds of actions. But I trust that my people will learn from their own experiences —the spirit of the illustrious personage addressed the young traveler in this way.

—Feelings can lead us as individuals and as a society to wonderful places or undesired ones. One of the secrets of life is being able to make that decision consciously —was Glem's enlightened response.

—It is time for me to depart. I was very pleased with your company, my dear friend —said the reverend as his spirit dissipated into the space, bidding farewell.

—My gratitude will be eternal, great leader. Your ideology and your way of fighting have taught me profound lessons. It has been an extraordinary and unforgettable journey by your side —responded the traveler, deeply moved.

The young man took a moment to calm his heightened emotional state before tapping into his actor's training, and thus attuning himself to the next emotion that would guide him towards encountering the next character. In this way, once he deeply identified with a sensation of mental expansiveness, his body smoothly flowed into a new place.

A GENIUS

Suddenly, the traveler found himself in the dining room of a cozy house, where a couple and their two children were enjoying dinner. At that moment, the young boy, around four years old, turned to his parents and said, *"The soup is too hot."* The two adults reacted with extreme surprise, asking the little one why he hadn't spoken before if he obviously knew how to speak. The child replied, *"Because everything was fine before."* And so, after smiling in Glem's direction as a gesture of welcome, he continued to blow on every spoonful before bringing it to his mouth.

The traveler found himself in the presence of an unusual little boy, as the prominent size of his head did not seem proportionate to the rest of his small body. In addition, his calm and introverted behavior was quite different from that of other children his age.

Shortly thereafter, the young traveler kept the solitary boy company in his room as he recovered from a cold. Suddenly, when his father approached and gifted him a compass, he was amazed to discover that the tiny needle always pointed to the same direction, regardless of the compass's position. At that moment, a keen interest in science was awakened in the young Albert Einstein.

As this character grew up, the traveler witnessed how much he enjoyed spending time in his father's workshop, who by then owned a company manufacturing and installing electrical equipment. Moreover, it was his uncle —who gifted him interesting books— that fostered his interest in science. It was precisely during this time that the future scientist began to develop his unique style of free thinking, engaging in deep questioning about various areas such as religion, the state, authority, and even science itself, in stark contrast to the traditionalist dogmas of the conservative society of that era.

During Albert's adolescence, the traveler observed moments where his weaknesses in humanities subjects were evident. In fact, on one occasion, his Greek teacher told him that judging by the quality of his work, he would never amount to anything in life —a statement that would later prove to be grossly mistaken—. In contrast, Albert excelled in mathematics and physics, even undertaking self-directed study of infinitesimal calculus. It was precisely due to this notable academic discrepancy that he failed his first attempt to enter the Swiss Federal Polytechnic in Zurich, and was required to attend tutorials to catch up on non-scientific subjects before gaining admission to the prestigious institution the following year. Around the same time, he also decided to renounce his German citizenship and proceeded to naturalize as a Swiss citizen, as his pacifist beliefs made him unwilling to fulfill German military service.

The traveler continued to accompany the character during his university years, witnessing the romance that blossomed with his fellow student Mileva Marić, a woman with a strong feminist and radical disposition. Eventually, the couple decided to get married three years after graduating.

Likewise, Glem witnessed with some astonishment how, after graduating, this brilliant character struggled to find a job in his field. The fact was that Einstein lacked experience and connections in the scientific community. So, thanks to a recommendation from a good friend, he obtained a job as a technical examiner at the patent office in Bern, Switzerland. Interestingly, this job provided him with decent financial stability as well as the opportunity to learn about a variety of inventions and technologies, proving to be a valuable experience for his later career.

He also had the time to dedicate himself to developing his most significant research, such as the studies of the Brownian motion of particles and the photoelectric effect, in addition to his greatest scientific legacy, the formulation of special relativity and the equivalence between mass and energy. Even the traveler, with an indescribable excitement transmitted by the notable physicist, witnessed how the first mentioned work earned him a doctorate degree from the University of Zurich, while the second made him worthy of the Nobel Prize in Physics.

However, by that time, he had already published his famous theory of relativity, but the jury decided not to take this impressive research into account because they did not fully comprehend it.

Furthermore, as an interesting complement, the traveler was pleasantly surprised when he discovered the artistic side of the scientist, who was a talented violinist. Einstein had been taking lessons since he was six years old, and it was common for him to carry his inseparable instrument, which he affectionately called "Lina," wherever he went. Remarkably, he was always willing to play the compositions of his favorite composers in front of friends or colleagues, and he even participated in some public and private concerts, as well as accompanying the organ in some synagogues.

—If I hadn't been a scientist, I would have loved to dedicate myself to music —the physicist told the young man in a reflective tone.

—Perhaps the world would have lost a brilliant mind and gained a formidable artist —replied the traveler honestly.

Throughout this intriguing journey, it was common for the young man to share with the character some of his leisure moments, such as taking long walks in the open air or sailing on a sailboat. During these activities, the scientist would engage in deep reflections about science and life itself.

—Look around you at all this immense wonder, my dear companion. Everything is God manifesting and experiencing Himself in everything and every being, with perfect synchronicity. For I conceive of a deity that is more akin to nature inherent in all creation, rather than to human-like beings —the scientist spoke to the traveler, making a clear allusion to the God he believed in, the same one proposed by the Jewish philosopher Baruch Spinoza, which antagonizes with the divinity adopted by many religions.

—I feel immensely surprised to discover how accurately we share the same idea of the Creator —was Glem's brief response, for whom that definition of God aligned perfectly with his Buddhist experience.

As for Einstein's love life, Glem observed how after sixteen years of marriage, that relationship deteriorated to the point where divorce was inevitable. However, a few months later, the famous scientist remarried, this time to his cousin, with whom he had been in a romantic relationship for seven years. The tireless traveler was constantly astonished, as the renowned scientist had up to six lovers —including Margarita, the alleged Russian spy—, during the time he was with his cousin Elsa.

Another characteristic of the scientist's personality that impressed the young man was the simplicity with which he lived. His bedroom could be compared to a monk's cell, with no paintings or carpets, and only the bare essentials for resting.

Furthermore, Einstein decided to change several of his habits after his second marriage. He resolved to never wear socks again, claiming that they only produced holes. His wardrobe was also very limited, consisting of a few shirts and trousers, all identical and of the same color. He believed that he preferred to use his brain for something more useful than deciding what to wear every morning.

This particular behavior made his new partner uncomfortable, and she even expressed to their friends that she regretted that Albert dressed up for his first wife but not for her.

In fact, on one occasion, the traveler couldn't contain his laughter when the distinguished scientist was caught by Elsa cutting the sleeves off a new shirt. When the lady confronted him and asked for an explanation, her husband simply stated that shirt cuffs required buttons or cufflinks and that they easily got dirty, so they had to be washed with care. He concluded by saying that *"all possessions are nothing but a stone tied to the ankle."*

Later, during his final journey, the traveler observed how the reputation of the distinguished scientist grew day by day. However, in Germany, the government systematically attempted to discredit his image. They even encouraged a group of Nazi students who, during a public event, decided to burn the physicist's books. Likewise, conferences were organized, which seemed more like media spectacles, where opinions were expressed to oppose the principles of the special theory of relativity. In this sense, the German authorities sponsored the publication of a book with a controversial title "One hundred authors against Einstein." When the character was asked about it, he simply replied *"Why one hundred? If I were wrong, one would be enough."*

In contrast, in the rest of the planet, Einstein's work was being passionately discussed with genuine scientific curiosity. Glem even witnessed a particular moment when, during an interview, a journalist asked Einstein if he could explain the theory of relativity to him in simple terms:

—Can you explain to me how to fry an egg? —Albert replied with another question.

—Of course, I can do it, dear professor! —confidently replied the reporter.

—Alright, but do it assuming that I don't know what an egg is, or a frying pan, or oil, or fire —concluded the physicist, leaving everyone present perplexed.

Similarly, during another pleasant dialogue with the press, the traveler witnessed an entertaining conversation. On this occasion, another journalist asked Einstein about the possible repercussions that his multiple nationalities may have had on his fame. To this, he responded with brilliance *"If my theories had turned out to be false, Americans would say I was a Swiss physicist, the Swiss would say I was a German scientist, and the Germans would say I was a Jewish astronomer."*

Some time later, just as had happened in previous travels, Glem observed how the panorama of that journey turned dark. The outbreak of the Second World War caused the scientist to partially abandon his pacifist nature. He considered that Germany had initiated the development of nuclear weapons, and this fact, along with a colleague, motivated him to write a letter to President Roosevelt, urging the United States to advance in the production of atomic bombs in order to promote an arms balance between the two nations. However, he was quite emphatic in his warnings about the enormous hazards of a nuclear war.

In this sense, the U.S. government initiated the Manhattan Project, which aimed to construct its first atomic weapons. However, Albert did not participate in the project, not even indirectly. At the end of the war, when the United States dropped atomic bombs on the Japanese cities of Hiroshima and Nagasaki, the distinguished physicist expressed deep sorrow over that tragic event.

—There are those who consider me the main promoter of the nuclear bomb, due to the correspondence I sent to the President along with a colleague. I find this to be a very unfortunate assessment, and not only unjust but also extremely superficial —Einstein confided to the traveler with deep sorrow.

—I trust that your image and legacy cannot be tarnished by anyone, intentionally or unintentionally. Your pacifist stance and scientific heritage are unquestionable —replied Glem with absolute honesty.

Furthermore, the traveler witnessed another remarkable moment in the life of the illustrious figure. Due to his close relationship with the Jewish people, and his years of collaboration in the establishment of the Hebrew University of Jerusalem, several leaders proposed him as the ideal replacement for the recently deceased Prime Minister of the newly formed state of Israel. They considered him "the greatest living Jew" and believed that he could likely solve the mathematical challenges of the economy and make them meaningful for the nation. However, Einstein immediately rejected the offer, stating that at the age of seventy-three, he did not feel capable of assuming such a responsibility. Moreover, his lack of political experience and limited relational skills could potentially hinder, rather than help, the country. He believed that it could adversely affect the valuable connection he had built with the Jewish people, which he considered his strongest human bond.

After all of this, Glem found himself in a room at the hospital in Princeton, New Jersey. Einstein, now seventy-six years old, had experienced internal bleeding caused by an abdominal aortic aneurysm. However, despite being in a state of perfect consciousness, he refused any surgical intervention, stating that he did not wish to artificially prolong his life.

—I want to decide when to depart. I feel like I've given everything I have. It was a pleasure to have your company, my young companion —Einstein spoke in this manner as his being faded away subtly.

—All the experiences I've had by your side are indescribable. The clarity of your teachings has allowed me to understand the world in a different way. I will be forever grateful —replied the traveler candidly.

At that moment, the ethereal body of the traveler returned to the time machine, thus concluding that stage of fascinating journeys filled with unforgettable experiences, a plethora of anecdotes, and profound learning. These experiences had brought about a new way of understanding reality and relating to the world in Glem's perspective.

THE MEETING

Once back in his routine, the young man's interactions with the various people who frequented the government building where the library was located, particularly with the parliamentarians, not only became more frequent, but he also gained a positive reputation. In every conversation, his astute analysis of the causes and consequences of the most notable global events made him particularly popular. In this regard, it was common for the brilliant young man to reference relevant historical events from his travels, providing a better perspective on current events and even predicting potential future events with great talent. Indeed, everyone who knew him agreed that with his intelligence and good preparation, he could aspire to high government positions. As for Glem, he always stated that he did not currently see himself in a political career, but he did not entirely dismiss that valuable recommendation, especially when he was aware that various people concurred with the same opinion.

Shortly thereafter, the young man received a call from his aunt's secretary, informing him that his aunt had arrived in the country and wished to speak with him over the phone.

—Dear Glem, I heard that you tried to reach out to me. I want to inform you that I have just returned from Europe, and in the next few days, while I recover from jet lag, I will be working from my home office. So if you wish to come and see me, I will be delighted to receive you —said the minister in this cordial manner as she addressed her nephew.

—Thank you aunt Lena. I will gladly come to visit you. How about this Friday?

—Let me check my schedule for a moment. ...Alright, I'll be expecting you on that day at three in the afternoon.

—Excellent, aunt Lena, I'll be there. Thank you for the call.

—It's always a pleasure to talk to you. See you soon.

At that moment, the young man hastened to organize his thoughts around the project that had been swirling in his mind, and through which he hoped to channel the emotions derived from his travels. He knew that if he could deliver a compelling presentation of his plan, he would likely have the support of the minister, just as had happened in the past.

In this way, the day arrived. Punctual as always, the young man knocked on the door and was immediately greeted by a courteous lady in an impeccable service uniform, who invited him to follow her to his aunt's office. Although Glem had been to that formidable mansion on one occasion in the past, his memories were vague.

It was during his parents' wedding reception when he was just five years old. What he did remember was that the most talked-about topic during that intimate gathering was the absence of the homeowner, the renowned Arthur Smith, who had cited a last-minute matter as an excuse without providing further details. However, everyone knew the real reason why he decided to skip the event, and that was because the former prime minister still harbored a remote hope of influencing his son to marry a woman from the circle of politically influential families in the country.

Once in the study, the lady greeted her nephew with an enthusiastic hug and invited him to sit down.

—Tell me, dear, what would you like to talk to me about?

—Do you remember the talk I gave some time ago, which you helped me to present at several universities? I would like to revisit the idea, but this time expands the content to cover more topics.

—Of course, I remember. People still occasionally mention how excellent those presentations were. But go on, tell me more. I am very interested in the topic.

—This time, I would like to give a conference that not only talks about passion, but also includes four other qualities: innovation, originality, leadership, and amplitude (open-mindedness). I also want to associate these qualities with famous historical figures, so as to describe each term in the best possible way.

—I love that project! And where would you like to present it? Again at universities and colleges in the province?

—This time, I would like to reach out to other spaces, such as the various centers that bring together the growing immigrant community. Because I think it would be a kind way to welcome them as they adapt to Canadian society. Moreover, it would allow me to continue delivering this conference for a longer period of time. That's why I wanted to know if you could support me in implementing the program.

—But obviously! You can count on my assistance. It seems like a valuable idea to add to our cultural programs targeted at different immigrant groups. And tell me, have you thought of a name for the talk?

—I've come up with something like "Discovering Values"

—I like the overall concept of what you've presented, but may I make a suggestion?

—That's exactly why I'm here, aunt, for your guidance.

—I believe that since the program is primarily aimed at adults, it may not be entirely accurate to say that we're going to discover new values. Instead, I think it would be more reasonable to say that we can awaken some values that may be dormant within us.

—I think that clarification is spot on. "Awakening Values" is a great title.

Afterwards, both of them, clearly excited about this interesting idea, continued discussing the potential scope of the project, how to shape it to be as effective as possible, and also defining which community could be the first to be presented with a pilot plan. In this regard, Glem decided to initially approach the large Asian community that continuously arrives in Canada, starting particularly with his Filipino compatriots, as he knew he would feel very comfortable in those surroundings.

After an hour, the minister received an important call, and at that moment the young man knew that the productive meeting had come to an end. He said a quick but warm goodbye to his aunt and left the office. Suddenly, the gracious lady who had greeted him at the door of the house intercepted him, kindly asking him to accompany her. The young man, somewhat puzzled, followed her, and a moment later found him at the doors of another office, when he immediately heard a voice that said forcefully:

—Come in and close the door —Mr. Arthur Smith addressed the boy sternly.

Glem obeyed the order and entered the very elegant office, closing the door as requested, and stood a few meters away from it.

—Approach and take a seat —his grandfather spoke to him in the same tone, while picking up the phone to signal his assistant not to be interrupted—. Do you know who I am?

—I know very well who you are, my father's father —Glem replied curtly.

The fact was that, for the boy, the word "grandfather" was associated with affection, being present, and sharing pleasant moments, in short, with familial love. A sentiment that he couldn't express towards that character, as it was the first time they exchanged words in their lives. Although it was true that they had coincided in few events, the former prime minister always managed skillfully to avoid being close to Glem and his mother. Even during Glem Smith's heartfelt funeral, the illustrious politician, without any sensitivity at all, sent his condolences to Ada and her son through his assistant.

—I am pleased to know that you are aware of the correct term for our relationship. And it is precisely with regard to this matter that I wanted to meet with you. It has come to my attention that for some reason, you have become a very popular person within the parliamentary complex. And that is why I am demanding that if you are using my last name to gain notoriety, you stop doing so immediately —Arthur concluded with extreme clarity and severity.

At that moment, as the old politician finished speaking, a myriad of arguments —mostly not very elegant ones—, started forming in the boy's head to respond to that arrogant character. And just when he was about to reply with absolute vehemence, something happened that left him paralyzed.

On the wall behind his grandfather, hanging in a special place, was a small square plank identical to the one his father had, with the thin mariner's rope unfurling from one of its ends and the same five words written on small gleaming plates. In that moment, he realized —to his immense surprise—, that the origin of those words that had guided the destiny of his fantastic journeys came from that particular person. So, after a brief reflection, he thought that if he allowed himself to express the behavior he had imagined for years, it would mean that all the lessons and growth experiences obtained during his travels would have been meaningless. Thus, with a calm attitude, he addressed his interlocutor:

—First and foremost, allow me to introduce myself, as unlikely as it may seem, we have never formally met. I am Glem Suárez, and I am proud to say that I have only one name and one surname, and it is not Smith. The most precious inheritance my father left me was his love and teachings for life, not the reputation of a surname. Furthermore, although I have not heard any kind words from you since I've been in your presence, such as "please come in," "if you would be so kind as to close the door," or "thank you for taking a seat," which is rather surprising coming from a politician of your stature, I sincerely appreciate the opportunity you have given me to meet with you.

I also want to be honest in saying that for years I imagined this moment would come, when we would sit down to talk. And although I have rehearsed many times what I would say in this situation, something unexpected has happened in this moment that has made me drastically change my mind. So, I will simply say that, for better or for worse, I have not had the opportunity to get to know you. I understand that it doesn't make much sense for me to form feelings towards you based on the experiences of other people, no matter how close they may be to me. Their conflicts, experiences, and ghosts are not mine. And I also want to tell you that despite my young age, I have had certain experiences that have taught me valuable lessons, and one of them is to understand that hatred is a feeling as baseless as it is useless, as it consumes the one who experiences it without affecting the target of that feeling.

As for the popularity you mentioned, I invite you to activate your network of collaborators and investigate more deeply into the matter, and then you will discover that the merits I have earned are not at all related to you or your surname. I can assure you that everyone who knows about our relationship has learned about it from third parties, as for me, that fact, despite what some people may think, does not add any value to me. —with these words, the young man concluded with astonishing composure.

On his part, the seasoned politician was disarmed by his grandson's attitude and words. But what surprised him the most was seeing a vivid reflection of his son in the young man, when many years ago, his son had confronted him to express his desire to forge his own path, determined to distance himself from the life plan that had been imagined for him. Moreover, he was very curious about one of the phrases uttered by the young man, so he decided to ask him:

—I must confess, young man, that you have impressed me, and that's not an easy thing to do. Moreover, I would like to know what unexpected event you mentioned that made you change your attitude towards me —spoke the old man, genuinely intrigued.

—Well, Mr. Smith, I don't know if you're aware, but my father kept a similar plaque to the one hanging on your wall with great reverence. I assume it was you who gifted it to him. The fact is, he lived according to those values, and now I have also decided to cultivate them. So, when I saw that object prominently displayed among your belongings, I understood that my father, in some way, always paid tribute to your teachings, and now, without even knowing it, I find myself continuing the same legacy —responded Glem with great maturity.

—Thank you, young man, for your honesty. It's been a long time since I received such a profound lesson as the one you've given me today. I take this opportunity to apologize for my behavior over all these years, and I ask you to convey my apologies to your mother as well —expressed Arthur Smith, with a humility that was uncharacteristic of his personality.

—I will do so. With your permission, it's time for me to leave. There's no need to call the kind lady, I know the way well —said Glem as he made his way towards the door of the spacious house.

On the way, he crossed paths with his aunt Lena again, who had noticed him leaving his father's office and asked:

—Is everything alright, son?

—Yes, aunt. I'm just much more relieved now —replied the young man, briefly pausing his stride to answer her before continuing on his way and leaving the place.

Shortly after, Lena quickly made her way to her father's office to find out what had happened during the unexpected meeting. As she entered the room, she asked:

—Father, has something happened? —the lady was surprised and intrigued.

—Yes, daughter. I have discovered that I have a grandson —was the unexpected response from the reserved man, whose face showed the sorrow of having missed precious moments in his life.

—It's good to know that you've found out. And, as you've always told me, it's never too late to do the right thing —said Lena Smith as she turned around and walked back to her own office.

Arthur Smith stayed put, contemplating what had happened in great detail. Then he remarked out loud to himself «Life has given me a new opportunity, even though it's not with my son but rather with my grandson. I don't want to throw it away».

CHAPTER V

THE NEW CONSCIOUSNESS

"A real and lasting peace in the world can only be possible, when each individual will experience genuine inner peace"

Once Glem started the presentation sessions for the conference "Awakening Values", initially aimed at the Asian immigrant community starting their lives in the province of Ontario, the reception exceeded expectations. Each talk turned into an engaging conversation where participants, with sincere admiration, appreciated the significant details that the young man mentioned about each character, following an impeccable chronology. Furthermore, these details were consistently focused on the value associated with each figure.

However, at the same time, the audience felt highly motivated to express their opinions, contributing valuable comments about different personalities from their culture, as well as sharing their own experiences that equally exemplified the virtues discussed in the captivating presentation. In this way, the activity always turned into an enriching exchange of ideas, encouraging the intellectual and spiritual growth of all attendees, but especially the speaker, who not only thoroughly enjoyed the work but also felt capable of fully controlling their emotions.

Before long, and as expected, the popularity of that presentation became so significant that Glem soon found himself overwhelmed with commitments. In light of this, his aunt, upon learning of the situation, decided to get in touch with him:

—Hello dear nephew, I have been informed about the success of your talks, as well as the numerous requests that have come up. Tell me, have you thought about how to handle this situation? —in this way, the minister spoke to him over the phone.

—Dear aunt, it's great to hear from you. That's right, and I must confess that I was pleasantly surprised by the excellent reception the presentation has received. I also want to let you know that I already have a plan to handle the situation. I have decided to temporarily pause the presentations in order to focus on training other facilitators who can assist me in spreading the workshop —the brilliant young man replied.

—I think it's a very wise action. I have full confidence that, as always, you will carry out this task with great success. Moreover, you know that you can count on me for anything you need.

—I know, aunt. And thank you for your valuable words of encouragement. I will keep you updated on my progress. Sending you a hug.

—Thank you, Son. Have a great day.

In this way, Glem dedicated himself to developing a comprehensive training program whose main objective was to attract the best human talent, so they could convey the content as if he were doing it himself. In this regard, the young man focused primarily on the ability of the presenters to connect with the audience with genuine passion. He knew that mastering the theoretical content of the project was always easier compared to the skill of positively impacting the audience.

During this new and challenging process, the young man felt especially fortunate to have his two good friends, Sandra Rizzi and Marcos Diaz, among the people interested in participating as presenters. Additionally, they were joined by a charming lady who was already familiar to Glem, the sharp and well-spoken Wendy Cortez. The communications between Marcos and the delightful guide from the Bell Museum became so frequent that a beautiful feeling blossomed between them, leading the girl to decide to relocate to the Canadian capital. These three candidates had already enjoyed the fabulous talk with immense pleasure, and they were captivated by the idea of being part of this wonderful project. As for the remaining two members to complete the group of five participants for the first training of speakers, they were connected to associations serving immigrant groups in the province of Ontario.

Once the instruction began, the dynamic devised by the young man to transmit his knowledge was brilliant. He created five detailed guides, both on the life of the character to be presented and the associated value. Each week, the participants were required to prepare with the assigned content, and then in a meeting, each one would give their presentation. During this presentation, everyone present would play the role of the audience, asking interesting questions and providing feedback in order to improve the skills of each facilitator. This dynamic would then be repeated for the necessary five weeks, allowing each member of the group to become acquainted with each value and character associated with the workshop.

A pleasant occurrence took place when, at the end of this enriching process, the participants expressed their deep gratitude to the young man for having invited them. This was because they all agreed that the training had tremendously positively impacted their lives.

—Thank you, my dear friend, for sharing your vision with me and the passion with which you carry out your projects. I hope that this valuable connection we have will endure forever —with eyes filled with pride, Sandra addressed her best friend.

—It is an immense pleasure for me to have your unwavering support in each of my crazy endeavors. As for me, I have no intentions of drifting away, so unless you decide otherwise, I hope you'll be willing to put up with me for much longer —Glem responded with a huge smile on his face.

In this way, time passed, and the new presenters, now integrated into the workshop's outreach program through immigrant support associations, expanded the program's reach. Soon, other communities had access to the engaging talk. Additionally, Glem divided his time between new training sessions and continuing to deliver his conference. Gradually, a beautiful group of supportive colleagues formed around the project led by the young man, and it continued to grow steadily.

It happened that on one occasion, Glem's three friends, Sandra, Marcos, and Wendy, requested a meeting with him on the following Monday. They wanted to discuss the possibility of assisting him in training new facilitators and exchanging ideas on the matter. The young man was immensely pleased with this extraordinary proposal and instantly confirmed his attendance to the appointment.

That Monday afternoon arrived, which happened to be November 11th, and it was the young man's twenty-first birthday. When he entered the training room where they had agreed to meet, he was surprised by a large group of people who shouted in unison, *"Happy Birthday, Glem!"* His friends had organized this surprise, and even during the preparations, they were pleasantly impressed by the number of people who spontaneously joined the celebration. This confirmed the immense appreciation that the young man had from everyone he knew.

During that emotional celebration, Glem felt deeply moved as he reunited with many loved ones and close friends. He shared the moment with his mother, aunt Lena, Mrs. Trembley, and the always pleasant Mya, along with many other acquaintances. The highlight of the evening came when Marcos unexpectedly pulled out his guitar and suggested that Ada join her son in singing their favorite piece, none other than the legendary "Imagine" by John Lennon. Both of them had beautiful voices that complemented each other perfectly. Just as they had done many times before, they captivated everyone present with a wonderful performance. As the song came to an end, the audience erupted in thunderous applause that filled the room, but suddenly, as they noticed the presence of a renowned figure, the entire hall fell into a sudden silence.

—I apologize for the interruption, as I am certain the applause was not meant for me —with such sarcasm, Arthur Smith addressed the surprised attendees—. I just wanted to approach and personally give a gift to my grandson.

—Thank you very much for the gesture, Mr. Smith —Glem, surprised, responded neutrally, while he received a wrapped package that appeared to contain a large and slim book, as well as a smaller and thicker one.

—Well, all that's left for me is to bid farewell to everyone present, wishing you all continued enjoyment of this pleasant celebration —Arthur said with the demeanor of a politician addressing his audience.

As the attendees saw the departure of that individual, they were perplexed by the fact that he had attended alone, without his usual group of collaborators, as if he had given the meeting a very private character. In that moment, the room remained silent as the minister took the floor to speak:

—Let's continue with the celebration! I'm sure there are many more songs that we all know —Lena spoke, encouraging all the guests.

Thus, the celebration resumed, and this time, the talented Marcos completely changed the genre to ignite the party. As he began to play, the lively Wendy invited the entire room to follow her lead and dance to the rhythm of "La Macarena."

Glem took advantage of that moment to retreat with his mother and aunt to a corner of the room, intending to open the enigmatic gift. As they uncovered it, they discovered an old family album along with a small but sturdy journal that had belonged to his father. The moment Lena saw the gift, she immediately said:

—That is the most precious family photo album of the Smiths and my brother's travel journal, which he carried everywhere before going to study in Vancouver. If my father gave them to you, it's because he truly considers you part of the family now. I propose that we gather one day to share the stories behind each memory —the minister spoke, a mix of curiosity and excitement in her voice.

—Well, no need to say more! We'll be waiting for you this Friday at home with a delicious Filipino dinner. And during the after-dinner conversation, you can share all about that intriguing past —responded Ada, feeling highly motivated by her sister-in-law's proposal.

After a few hours, the attendees started to leave, and when only the birthday boy, his mother, and the three organizers remained, the young man turned to Sandra.

—Dear friend, would you grant me the honor of accompanying me to dinner at our usual Italian restaurant? Let's continue the celebration —said Glem, while making a playful bow, as if he were portraying a character from Shakespeare's plays.

—By asking in such a charming manner, my dear gentleman, you have left me defenceless, so I find no reason to refuse —responded Sandra, as she crossed her legs and slightly curtsied, while her hands mimicked the opening of a long courtly gown.

All present burst into laughter at the impromptu performance by the young couple. At that moment, Ada suggested they go for dinner, assuring them she would take care of everything and close the venue. Marcos and Wendy kindly offered to help, allowing the two friends to feel free to leave.

A few minutes later, they arrived at "La Roma," where the always friendly Mrs. Maria warmly welcomed them, congratulated the young man, and then escorted them to a pre-booked table in a discreet corner of the restaurant. While they chatted and perused the menu, Sandra was surprised to hear, for the first time in that place, a trio of musicians. They were three charming elderly gentlemen who played a variety of Italian songs with great precision, accompanied by a violin, a guitar, and the ever-present accordion.

The evening was passing by in a very pleasant manner, so a moment after they had finished their meal, Glem raised his hand to call the musicians, and they promptly approached. Sandra, puzzled, looked at him intently and asked:

—Are you going to request a song?

—No, I'm going to do something better. I want to dedicate the following song to you, I hope you like it —he said, as he stood up from his seat and positioned himself next to the musicians.

In fluent Italian, thanks to his natural language skills and the many hours of practice he had invested with the hired trio of musicians, Glem performed a song by the popular Italian singer-songwriter Franco Battiato, titled 'La Cura' (The Cure). The lyrics were simply a beautiful declaration of love:

—I will protect you from the fears of hypochondria
From the disruptions you will encounter on your journey from today onwards
From the injustices and deceptions of your time
From failures that, due to your nature, you will normally attract
I will alleviate you from your pains and mood swings

I will free you from the obsessions of your quirks
I will overcome the gravitational currents
Space and light so you don't age
And you shall be healed from all illnesses
Because you are a special being
And I will take care of you....

As the passionate performance came to an end, Sandra, deeply captivated and with her emotions running high, couldn't hold back the tears that welled up spontaneously. The two friends knew each other so well, and in that moment, with just a glance, they recognized that they had always been in love with each other. At that moment, Sandra stood up from the table and, with a trembling voice, said to him.

—I also promise to take care of you, my love.

Glem reacted by embracing her tightly, and they shared a passionate kiss. In that moment, both individuals discovered what it meant to lose the sense of time and space for a moment. The musicians stepped back, and the lovely couple continued their conversation.

—Since when do you speak Italian so well? —asked the girl with admiration and intrigue.

—Well, I admit that I don't speak it. I just learned this song to dedicate it to you —he responded with honesty.

—And why did you choose that song? Did you know that Franco is my mother's favorite Italian singer? I have grown up listening to his music, so I have come to appreciate him.

—I didn't know! I just wanted to find a song that somehow expressed how I feel about you. And suddenly, I came across that wonderful lyric that talks about care, justice, nature, gravity, space, and light. It surprised me a lot, as if I had written it myself.

—I agree. It couldn't be more fitting to you and this new phase you're going through —replied to the young woman, as she took her companion's hands—. And tell me, why did it take you so long to express your feelings to me?

—I confess that, even though from the very beginning I knew that I felt more than a sincere friendship for you, I believed I wasn't ready to express it. For a long time, I chose to be a free soul with no major commitments. During that time, something wonderful happened: a beautiful and honest friendship grew between us. And now, as I decided to leave behind my wandering lifestyle and settle down, destiny gifted me with the marvelous opportunity to work together on the conference that we have enjoyed delivering so much. That's why, when you confessed that you shared my vision, my passion for projects, and that all of that made you feel our connection growing, I realized that I felt the same way. That's why I spent weeks rehearsing this fantastic song with these kind gentlemen, so I could surprise you by dedicating it to you today —Glem concluded with the satisfaction of someone who has fully achieved their objective.

—I'm delighted to know how much we coincide in everything you express. And I'm also happy that you took the initiative, especially on such a special occasion. Because if you hadn't acted soon, I had already decided to forget about Italian and Filipino customs and be the one to propose to you —Sandra said, with an ironic smile on her face—. I must admit that I sometimes had doubts whether I was the only one harboring these feelings of love, as throughout our faithful friendship, I didn't perceive any signs that you felt the same. Why did you choose to express it now?

—For some time now, as I started contemplating what I wanted my future to be like and, most importantly, the kind of person I envisioned sharing my life with, your image kept appearing in my mind. Furthermore, as suggested by Japanese tradition, if your partner also becomes your best friend, the relationship can endure over time because, in the autumn of our years, when the fervor of youth and the productivity of maturity have passed, we will value a splendid companionship more, someone with whom we can contemplate life, reminisce about good times, and pass on wisdom to future generations —pondered Glem, with great wisdom.

After leaving the restaurant, the lovely couple decided to spend the night together. During that sublime encounter, they surrendered themselves to an almost mystical experience. In that moment, they understood that the subconscious mind does not make mistakes, as they discovered they were meant for each other. Thus, with immense pleasure, the young couple not only confirmed their deep physical and spiritual connection, but also the fact that taking this step from a solid friendship placed them in a wonderful state of conscious love, bypassing the exhilarating yet often tumultuous stage of infatuation.

On Friday night, everything was ready, awaiting the arrival of the minister. Ada, Glem, and now Sandra had been preparing everything with special care since early in the day, so they were engaged in lively conversation in the living room when they heard a knock on the door. Upon opening it, Lena Smith entered, greeting everyone with great excitement, and as soon as she caught a whiff of the food, she remarked:

—Mmm... This delicious aroma feels familiar! Let me guess. Could it be Adobo? —spoke the lady with a good deal of certainty.

—That's right! And we made it with chicken. Your favorite! —Ada replied, knowing very well her sister-in-law's weakness for Asian food.

—Thank you, my dear Ada, for always spoiling me. I think it's about time I make up my mind and learn how to cook that dish I love so much.

—With pleasure, I'll share the recipe with you. It's very simple to make. Ask Sandra, who was involved in preparing the meal today.

At that moment, the smiling girl nodded her head and turned towards Lena.

That traditional Filipino dish, known as "Adobo" was prepared on this occasion using chicken —well, it can also be made with beef or pork— the main ingredient, after being marinated in vinegar, soy sauce, garlic, bay leaves, and black peppercorns, was slowly cooked until the meat was tender. On this occasion, it was served with a delicious "Pancit," which are rice noodles stir-fried with vegetables, prepared with great care by Ada. As a beverage, they served a delightful "Shake of Ube," which consists of cooked Purple Yam mixed with evaporated milk, condensed milk, crushed ice, and sugar, resulting in a sweet and thick drink with a light purple color, very popular in the Philippines.

After finishing dinner, everyone moved to the living room and sat around the delicate coffee table, where the photo album and journal of Glem Smith lay. But before opening those books, filled with so many memories, the young man spoke up:

—I wanted to let you all know that I decided to invite Sandra to join us in this intimate moment because, besides being my best friend, she has now become my girlfriend. And since she is now part of the family, I believe she deserves to be with us in this very special moment —Glem spoke as he hugged and kissed his partner.

—It was about time you two came clean. I think everyone around here knew that you loved each other, it was just a matter of you admitting it too —Lena exclaimed, raising her hands in a triumphant gesture.

—I am so happy for you, my beloved children. And I can only imagine the moment when I will have the most beautiful grandchildren in my arms —exclaimed Ada, with overflowing excitement.

After that conversation, the minister opened the album and began narrating the stories behind each photograph. Most of them depicted joyful family trips across the Canadian landscape. As they looked at the many portraits, they could see the transition of Glem and Lena from children to teenagers. And in each of those moments, there was the image of a beautiful lady, Mrs. Hellen Smith, Glem's paternal grandmother.

—Aunt, could you tell us about my grandmother? My father was always very reserved about that topic, so I know very little about her —asked the boy, with genuine curiosity.

—It will be a pleasure to tell you about my mother. As you can see in the photographs, she was a very beautiful woman. Tall, blonde, slender, and with the same sky-blue eyes as your father. During that time, we spent many happy moments traveling as a family. Usually, it was my mother, with Glem's help, who meticulously organized all our journeys. I have always been very close to my father, whereas my brother was completely devoted to our mother. They were the best companions, enjoying reading all kinds of books and then exchanging opinions. They also loved to walk, be in contact with nature, and go fishing together. Moreover, all those travel experiences, books, and profound conversations were captured by Glem in his inseparable journal.

However, when Mom was forty-three, she began to suffer from heart problems. By then, I had already gone to study at the University of Toronto, my brother was in high school, and my father was completely absorbed in his political life. Her health deteriorated, and we didn't notice it. However, when my brother sensed that something serious was happening because our mother no longer felt capable of doing the activities they had always enjoyed together, he went to alert my father to take urgent action. But the busy Arthur Smith merely asked his wife how bad she felt, and she, not wanting to worry the family, replied that it was nothing serious and that she would find a solution to her health problem by contacting the necessary specialists. That simple response was enough for Arthur —unlike how he handled his work matters— not to dig deeper into the issue and not to insist regularly enough on the subject.

At first, my mother tried to take care of everything necessary to seek a cure, but she gradually realized that her health was deteriorating rapidly. Understanding that she was alone in a relentless race against time, she decided to live the remaining days in a full and simple way. After two years, she passed away peacefully after suffering a heart attack. My brother was deeply affected, and when the doctors indicated that it would have been possible to help her if we, as a family, had dedicated ourselves to exhaust all available resources, Glem believed that it was our father who chose his job over his wife's health. From that moment on, an insurmountable abyss emerged between those two individuals.

After the death of our mother, Glem decided to go to the other side of the country to study merchant marine as a way to distance himself from our father and the landscapes that reminded him so much of her. He also chose to abandon his precious journal, in which Hellen Smith usually appeared as the main character of each story. As for my father, after being widowed and perhaps as a way to deal with his grief and, who knows, with a certain sense of guilt for his indifference during his wife's convalescence, he devoted himself even more to working in politics. It was not surprising that he soon became the leader of his party, and when they won the elections, he took office as the prime minister. As for me, once I graduated with a degree in "Public Administration and Politics", my dad asked me to work by his side. Without much thought, I accepted his proposal, and since then, I haven't known any other world than politics.

—Thank you so much, aunt Lena, for sharing all these wonderful stories with us. Now I can understand so much about the past, and I finally have a clearer picture of my grandmother. I will cherish this day deeply in my memory —spoke Glem, clearly moved.

—I also thoroughly enjoyed this evening. Thank you, my beloved family, for the invitation —concluded the minister, while giving a heartfelt hug to each one of those present.

At that moment, the emotional gathering came to an end, leaving the hosts noticeably impressed by the wealth of information they had learned about the unique Smith family.

In the following days, as expected, the young man eagerly read every page of his father's logbook. He enjoyed every one of the tales, as if reading a thrilling adventure novel. It confirmed the striking resemblance he shared with his father, not only in terms of their personalities but also their ability to narrate captivating stories.

After some time had passed, the day arrived when Glem began his university career. Sandra wanted to accompany her boyfriend, and along the way, she shared the motivations behind her decision to study psychology, as well as her experiences during her recent first year of study at the prestigious Carleton University in Ottawa.

—Now tell me, why did you choose that profession? —Sandra asked her partner.

—Well, when I was deciding what to study, I came across the synopsis of this career and I immediately knew it was what I was looking for —Glem replied, while showing her the interesting summary.

Sandra took the paper and began to read it carefully: "Are you interested in the environmental, economic and sociopolitical challenges that humanity faces at the onset of the 21st century? Do you want to better understand how and why some countries "develop" (and others do not) in a world of globalizing markets, new technologies and ideas? Are you drawn to issues such as human rights, poverty reduction, climate change, humanitarian crises, social and corporate responsibility, fragile states and the education and health of "vulnerable" populations? Do you want to learn how humanity can find both fair and lasting solutions to such problems? The Honours bachelor's in international development and Globalization combines' theory and practice within a rigorous academic program and provides students with field experience through work and study terms in Canada and abroad."

—Well, I don't think there could be a better career for you. It's like you wrote that summary yourself —commented Sandra, proud of the decision her boyfriend had made.

—I'm sure our children will have the perfect balance at home, a level-headed psychologist and a crazy dreamer —Glem replied, as they both laughed at that remark.

As expected, the young man's university years were progressing extraordinarily. He quickly earned the admiration of his peers and the appreciation of his professors, as he often contributed brilliant ideas during the evaluation of various case studies, demonstrating an excellent analytical ability.

An example of his talent was evident during the study of a highly significant event that occurred earlier that year. A professor asked the students to analyze the various manifestations that arose because of the decision of the US and a group of allies to invade Iraq in order to put an end to —according to reports from US intelligence— with the production of chemical weapons and to achieve the establishment of a democratic regime in the country.

Several students pointed out noteworthy data regarding the issue, among which were the numerous demonstrations that took place in approximately six hundred cities around the world, against the intervention. They particularly emphasized the protest in Rome, which gathered the historic figure of three million people. They also highlighted the fact that the UN did not support that military operation, as its experts had determined that at that time, the Iraqi government was not developing weapons of mass destruction.

On his part, Glem took the floor and, capturing the attention of his classmates, expressed his opinion:

—I believe that wars often stem from various motivations, which are usually different from the limited reasons put forward by politicians who incite conflicts. In this case, considering that the US was experiencing its highest fiscal deficit in decades, it is possible that the government saw an opportunity to employ a familiar strategy: to stir up nationalism in order to divert the population's attention towards that particular issue. Additionally, they may have hoped that a wartime economy and potential influence over oil prices, as seen at the end of the Persian Gulf War, would aid in their economic recovery. However, it seems that several factors spiraled out of their control. Firstly, public opinion in the US became deeply divided, unlike ever before in response to a military conflict involving the country. Similarly, as previously mentioned, there was a precise coordination of unprecedented global protests, thanks to the effective use of the internet. This leads me to believe that in the future, we will be able to organize ourselves as virtual communities of citizens to express our opinions, without relying solely on traditional media channels —the young man affirmed, making an accurate prediction—. On the other hand, once again, it became evident the limited authority exerted by the UN in the face of the power of certain governments, sadly turning it into an instrument to be manipulated according to the convenience of certain powers. And finally, I will mention what, in my opinion, was the most misguided calculation, which is that the allied side believed that by having the most advanced military technology, the effectiveness of the invasion and the swift resolution of the conflict would be guaranteed. However, as we have come to know, the entire scenario has turned into a brutal unconventional war, in which numerous Islamic guerrillas, taking advantage of the characteristics of the country's geography and the deeply anti-Western Arab culture, have generated immense chaos that often surpasses the maneuvering and control capacity of the invading forces. The most regrettable aspect is the number of civilians and soldiers who continue to die in a war whose official justification has been clearly refuted, as the nonexistence of the chemical and biological weapons supposedly developed by Saddam Hussein's dictatorial government has been publicly confirmed —in this way, Glem concluded his brilliant intervention, while his classmates expressed their full agreement with his arguments.

During his four years of study, the young man effortlessly excelled in all his academic activities, consistently demonstrating remarkable intelligence. He easily earned the affection of all his professors, becoming the favorite student of the faculty teaching international economics, global politics, development studies, and environmental sustainability. As a result, when it came time for his internships, this group of professors suggested that he pursue them at the 'Center for International Development and Globalization Research,' which operates within the University of Ottawa itself. This center is dedicated to multidisciplinary research, the study and analysis of international development, and topics related to globalization, always promoting academic research and the dissemination of knowledge in this field. In doing so, it serves a wide range of both public and private organizations.

And it was precisely this broad scope that motivated the young man to choose the option proposed by the professors, despite having several other alternatives, including government-affiliated organizations.

ESSAY

As soon as he started his activities at the center, he participated in an interesting study aimed at examining the causes of international conflicts. Upon successfully completing his work, he was praised by everyone he interacted with, but especially in recognition of his accomplishment —of his own initiative— of an original essay. Glem, with extraordinary creativity, crafted an outstanding piece of writing, which he decided to develop as a work of fiction, featuring a protagonist —a renowned historian—, unexpectedly, embarks on a journey to the future, where he discovers, amazed, that humanity had finally achieved living in complete peace and harmony. This was the approach devised by the brilliant young man to present a series of principles that he believed could help reduce conflicts in the world. This unique story was the result of masterfully capturing the experiences accumulated in his time travels, as well as the many books he enjoyed reading and the valuable knowledge gained during his academic education.

That magnificent essay earned the distinction of being published by the university, becoming a reference for the new cohorts of students in the "International Development and Globalization" program. Thus, in the faculty library, interested individuals could access the following narrative:

"Humanity without Wars

The renowned English historian, Mell Thomas, descended to the basement of his house in search of an old monograph he had written about the evolution of political systems from the middle ages to the present. As he approached the closet where he kept a large collection of his works and other seldom-used items, he noticed a faint light seeping out from between the closed doors. Intrigued, he quickened his pace, knowing that the old wardrobe had no internal lighting, leading him to suspect that someone had left a flashlight inside. Standing in front of the wooden cabinet, he swung open both doors simultaneously, only to be immediately blinded by a brilliant white light. Suddenly, he felt his body being pulled towards a wide and expansive tunnel, with a glimpse of an exit visible at the far end.

The sexagenarian decided not to resist and allowed himself to be carried by an unknown force, levitating through the passage until he emerged on the other side, which appeared to be a sort of time portal.

When he emerged from the tunnel, he found himself in a beautiful square filled with lush trees, surrounded by a series of magnificent buildings that harmoniously blended with the stunning vegetation of the place. It was like the perfect combination of a modern city nestled in a tropical forest.

At that very moment, feeling somewhat bewildered by that supernatural experience, which resembled more of a lucid dream, he noticed an enchanting lady approaching. She was elegantly dressed in business attire, and her age seemed to be contemporaneous with his own. As they stood face to face, she addressed him, saying:

—Welcome, Professor Thomas. Please follow me —spoke the enigmatic lady as she gestured for him to follow.

—But where am I? Who are you? Where are we going? How do you know my last name? —asked the academic, completely bewildered.

—All your questions will be answered; I just ask that you hurry your steps. The portal won't be open forever. So, we must make the most of our time.

That clear response made the old professor feel somewhat reassured, so he decided to obey and walk at her pace. Soon, they entered a beautiful and modern building, and then they found themselves in an elegant office, with the most remarkable feature being its ceiling filled with long, thin lines of lights. Once they both sat down, the historian asked again.

—Where am I?

—You are on Earth, but in the year 2911.

—And how did I get here?

—For us, with the current knowledge and technology, it is quite simple to create portals in time.

—But why specifically me?

—We have transported many like you. Influential individuals of your time who also possess the sensitivity to comprehend the events of our history.

—Oh! I am here because I am a historian.

—That is one of the reasons, although not the main one. But to optimize the limited time we have, allow me to begin my explanation —the lady said, as she manipulated the bracelet on her left hand, and immediately a series of lights from the ceiling formed a virtual screen in front of both.

—Alright, I'm all ears —replied to the professor, amazed as he observed the holographic projection.

—My name is Dinna, I am one of the individuals responsible for the temporal contacts program, and the purpose of this meeting is to inform you about the process of evolution that we have undergone to reach our current level of consciousness.

During the 2020s, the most feared and painful event in human history occurred, the outbreak of the Third World War, but this time it was a nuclear conflict —the lady spoke as a series of images depicting the conflict appeared on the screen—. It was a devastating event, and several territories in the northern hemisphere of the planet were ravaged by the detonation of atomic bombs during that absurd war. Now, at this point in my story, I am about to detail the five stages that led us from that fateful moment to the present day.

After that terrible incident, as expected, the world plunged into immense chaos. The detonations of those nuclear weapons instantly caused an incalculable number of deaths due to intense radiation. Many others would die shortly after due to burns caused by the explosions themselves, as well as multiple uncontrolled fires in various areas. In addition, the collapses of buildings and other disasters quickly increased the death toll. And if all of this wasn't enough, the already disrupted climate showed even more severe effects. Torrential rains and strong winds spread the radioactive contamination beyond the epicenter of the detonations, making it challenging for specialized rescue teams to risk their lives in such extreme circumstances. Furthermore, the mass displacement of survivors to safer areas created a significant humanitarian crisis.

Soon after, the financial systems collapsed, and the global political leadership lost all credibility and authority, leaving the armed forces of several nations without direction. Traditional media outlets ceased to be reliable sources of information, leading society to organize itself and create its own networks for information exchange. Chaos ensued, with people worldwide primarily struggling to obtain food and basic supplies for survival.

Subsequently, a few months later, groups of people rallied around an independent scientific community that proved to be detached from the power dynamics of the recent past. Once the levels of residual radiation permitted, they embarked on an exhaustive phase of assessing the damage, known as the "Diagnosis" stage. They were able to determine the state of the areas where the bombs had detonated, as well as the conditions of some survivors. The picture they encountered was utterly devastating. Once the radioactive materials settled in the affected areas and their surroundings, a strong contamination affected the soil, water, crops, and buildings, essentially the entire environment. Consequently, several cities became the most depopulated and inhospitable places on the planet. As for the people, evidence of radiation-related illnesses emerged, for which there were no known treatments at that time.

—Could you please provide more details about that war? What caused it? Which countries were involved —Mell asked, deeply impacted by the images he was witnessing.

—I am not authorized to disclose those details. However, that is not the most relevant aspect. What is essential here is for you to understand the process that led us to our present —replied the lady as she continued with her narrative—. After that sad first stage, the "Review" phase followed. The different systems of government, economy, and social organization were put under a rigorous examination, with the aim of identifying successes as well as our greatest mistakes, and using this analysis as a starting point to foster a true human change. During this stage, scientists were accompanied by the world's leading academic authorities and other renowned leaders, none of whom belonged to the political or religious sphere. The goal was not only to deeply examine the systems that had governed the world, but also to propose new models that would promote harmonious coexistence and, consequently, the end of wars.

—I must admit that I feel like I'm listening to a science fiction story. I can't imagine a world where politicians and the powerful, who have always dominated the planet, surrender and hand over control to another group —interrupted the historian, completely bewildered.

—I never said that one group handed control over to another. What actually happened was that, despite the attempts of those in power to maintain their hegemony, the catastrophic conditions at that time led the vast population to trust those who provided results rather than excuses and promises. Generally, scientists are reserved individuals who speak less, and it makes sense for them to be that way. If they conduct an experiment and succeed, they simply present the results, which speak for themselves. On the other hand, if they attempt something and fail, they have nothing to say. They learn from the mistake and continue to explore new ways to solve the problem at hand. In contrast, politicians are the opposite. They are always talking, and even when they fail, that's when they talk the most. The same can be said of religious leaders.

Furthermore, another point in favor of the group of scientists and engineers who stepped forward in those dark hours is that, for the first time, society felt treated with honesty and transparency. Without reservation, they dedicated themselves to disseminating and making available to the global population all inventions that proved useful in getting out of that chaotic situation. At the same time, they worked to ensure the functioning of the necessary technological infrastructures for communities to survive. Likewise, in this juncture where money lost its intrinsic value, everything shifted towards a more cooperative society, governed mainly by the exchange of goods and services and the sincere collaboration of individuals for the common good.

In such a way, this group meticulously analyzed the reasons that led to the war, instantly reaffirming well-known conclusions that had been discussed for years. It was clear that the hierarchy of values on which humanity had relied for centuries was completely misguided. For instance, it was common for individuals to express their desire to create a better life, both for themselves and their families. But in the 21st century, what did a better life mean? At that time, this concept primarily referred to having more money, power, sex, possessions, and other material and ephemeral things. However, after the events unfolded and unquestionably demonstrated that the greatest experiences and creations of humanity were directly influenced by the level of consciousness, both individual and collective, they understood that the solution had to come from the spiritual realm, but not in a religious sense. They fostered an elevation of consciousness in all individuals, which would redefine the notion of a better life as the deepest and most marvelous experience of being in perfect connection with one's surroundings.

—Very interesting! All of this reminds me of the quote by Albert Einstein that says, «No problem can be solved from the same level of consciousness that created it» —added Thomas with great relevance.

—Excellent remark! It was a great pleasure for us when we had the visit of the notable physicist —pleased, Dinna replied, quickly picking up the thread of her presentation—. Now, after the arduous process of self-evaluation, which was not devoid of intense debates, conflicts over control of the discussions, and attempts to impose different ideas, everything gradually leaned towards an almost unanimous proposal: to initiate the immense change required through a profound transformation of both the process and purpose of the global educational model.

This was the third stage addressed, the "Education" stage. Everyone involved knew that it would take several generations to achieve the expected results, but it was necessary to start at some point, and that moment of great devastation presented itself as the starting point to embark on the path towards a new teaching framework that prioritized wisdom over mere knowledge.

—Your approach sounds great. What was this new system based on? —the professor spoke, intrigued.

—Well, in the proposed new educational structure, students wouldn't be told what they should know or what is true, but instead, how they should arrive at their own truth. For centuries, the transmitted knowledge mainly focused on developing individual memory rather than fostering discernment. For instance, in the context of history, people were asked to remember facts, data, or events, which carried a significant cultural bias. Each teaching heavily depended on the era and society delivering it, but it fell far from providing individuals with pure and simple truth. In the past, narratives didn't represent what actually happened but rather a convenient interpretation of events by those in positions of power and control. They described events in the most favorable way for themselves. In this regard, what was taught wasn't history at all but rather politics.

—But knowledge is necessary. Without it, we would practically have to start discovering everything anew in each generation —interrupted Mell, with genuine concern.

—Your argument is very valid. That's why I must clarify that the implemented system did not eliminate the transmission of knowledge, which is indeed necessary, especially in the field of sciences. Instead, it proposed to limit it to what is strictly necessary. Let's go back to the example of studying history for a moment. With this new model, teachers describe events exactly as they happened, including all the facts and perspectives of those involved on both sides of the analyzed situation. That's why in this case, asking students to memorize dates, figures, or data is meaningless. Instead, they are told, "We have already transmitted all the available knowledge on this matter to you. Now, based on this, what do you think? What wisdom can you attain? What would you do if a similar scenario were presented to you, based on all the information provided? How would you act? Do you feel that you could learn from the past and thus build a different future?" This way, this new teaching framework recognizes that knowledge can be lost, but wisdom endures forever.

On the other hand, everyone knew that the outcome of an educational system with such characteristics, in which critical thinking was particularly privileged, would ensure that in the future societies would be governed by the best leaders.

—That's such a fascinating concept. I would love to learn more about it —the historian commented, clearly excited.

—Everything in due time and at its own pace, my dear professor —replied the composed lady, continuing the conversation—. Alongside everything that has been proposed, the fourth phase was set in motion, called 'Reconstruction.' It not only referred to the infrastructure of countries severely affected during the conflict but focused particularly on the inner aspect of the beings residing in each individual on the planet. The initial approach in this stage was to invite the global society to behave like one big family and then strive to go beyond that, fostering a genuine sense of unity among all of humanity. The powerful premise put forth explained that whatever good we do for one person, we do for all, and conversely, when we inflict suffering upon an individual or group, it is practically impossible for us to feel well because it is something we do to ourselves and to the rest of beings. These proposals, given the circumstances and in response to the spontaneous acts of solidarity that emerged to alleviate the many post-war needs, were received with great openness.

—But how marvelous everything you're telling me sounds! I could have never imagined that mankind could have evolved to such a state of consciousness in less than a millennium —said the professor, feeling perplexed.

—Perhaps what is difficult for you to conceive is the immense potential for change that can be triggered by a nuclear annihilation —she responded as she continued to display more recent images of the way of life in the new global community—. And finally, we reached the fifth and final stage, which we called the "New Consciousness" This stage involved establishing and maintaining, although after a tremendous amount of work and effort, an evolved way of life. So, I will now show you several characteristics of our current society. One of the most significant achievements is that we have finally been able to eradicate conflicts and wars.

An important attribute that defines this new society is that we have internalized that the world we live in, as well as our experience of it, is a reflection of both the individual and collective consciousness of all the inhabitants of the planet. We have understood that unity fosters active compassion towards all beings, which means collaborating so that everyone can progress through their own means. Furthermore, a global community ensures the efficient distribution of all resources and global wealth among individuals. This way, each person obtains the basic necessities to live with dignity, and no one feels the need to take something away from another person.

—Everything you're telling me sounds like the communist manifesto. I can't believe that's the governing system you live in! What happened to competition and the free market that drove economic development in the world? —asked the professor, genuinely surprised by what he had just heard.

—Our system of self-governance is far from being a communist model, so let me explain. The communist manifesto you mentioned declared that all individuals were equal, and as a result, government leaders would be responsible for the equitable distribution of resources, ensuring equality even through force if necessary. This concept is flawed from its ideological foundation, as individuals are not born, grow, or develop as equals. Moreover, the moment a group assumes the task of controlling the system, the foundational principle is already broken, as those in charge of distribution will always have greater and better access to the goods to be administered. On the contrary, it is entirely false to say that we are all equal, and that is perfectly fine. It is in diversity that the richness of life resides, with individuality and the ability to express it fully giving meaning to existence. In our society, equality is understood differently. It refers to the fact that everyone, without exception, is equal before the law and guaranteed the same opportunities to pursue their life purposes.

—This is all so fascinating! In fact, I've heard of several utopian systems like the one you describe. But I have a question: How did human beings manage to build such a high-order society?

—I'll tell you, it has been centuries of work and transformation, of trying out ideas, patiently waiting for results to emerge, and then evaluating and correcting. Along the way, we realized that whenever any doubt arose, the best strategy in each case was to ask ourselves: What is the most loving decision we can make? By doing so, we knew that we could always choose the best possible alternative. In this manner, we foresaw that true change would occur when we devoted ourselves, with special care, to nurturing the seeds.

By this, I mean precisely the upbringing of each individual in society, from their early age until they became adults. And it was precisely when we focused on nurturing the best individuals, with strong values, critical thinking, and a passion for discovering their life's mission that we paved the way to reach the point where we are today.

—I have always been convinced that education holds the key to change. But what did you do differently to achieve such a lofty goal?

—Well, let me explain. The fact is that we designed an innovative system of comprehensive education, supported by the concept of a global family and with love as the main component. Children do not start formal schooling until the age of eleven. During this time, they stay with their parents, grandparents, or attend pre-school centers. Strong values are instilled in them while they engage in play; explore their interests in arts, sports, science, and other facets. They also learn to read, write, and acquire basic math skills. But once they reach the age to enter the formal education system, their family members must make one of the most important decisions in any child's life: choosing their teacher from that moment until they turn twenty-two, which marks the completion of the entire educational process. In this way, children are grouped into cohorts of eleven individuals, and from there, they embark on a wonderful adventure.

—But with that model, a large number of teachers will be needed to cater to the entire student population of the world.

—You are correct in your observation, professor. But you would be amazed to know that there are always more candidates willing to become teachers than there are available positions for this noble profession. And this doesn't mean that the requirements to become a teacher are easy; in fact, it is a position that demands the highest qualifications in society, being the most demanding and prestigious profession on the planet. For instance, one of the requirements is that the minimum age to work as a comprehensive teacher is sixty-five years old.

—But that's the retirement age in my time!

—Yes, I know. However, we understood that only someone who has lived long enough and has demonstrated that they have done so fully and with integrity deserves the trust to guide the new generations. We also believe that anyone between the ages of twenty and sixty is still learning to live, discovering so many things, and trying to find their exact place in the world, so it would be a great mistake to give them such a high responsibility. Furthermore, this person must have solid experience, in such a way that they are capable of fully answering the various questions and concerns that arise during this long and fascinating teaching process. Additionally, they need to be free from any commitments that could hinder the proper performance of their work, as it is a full-time job. The student generally moves to a school house and lives there for eleven years with their teacher and classmates. In this sense, the whole group creates a strong brotherhood and a deep connection with their teacher, conditions that endure forever.

—Does that mean that parents are not present for some of the best moments of their children?

—Parents are free to visit their children whenever they want and for as long as they consider necessary, or as you mentioned, be present for the most significant moments in their children's lives. They can even have their children stay overnight at their homes, although they usually come to understand that it's more convenient for everyone if they live on the school campus. The fact is, parents themselves were educated under this system, and therefore, they perceive it as the natural process of things. Additionally, even these school houses become temporary residences because the teacher, throughout the entire duration of the education, travels with their group of students around the world. The purpose of this practice is to provide students with the best possible scenario for optimal learning on any subject. For example, if they are going to study the seasons and different types of climates on the planet, a journey is planned that will last as long as the teacher deems necessary. During this journey, the group will travel to different places where they can directly experience each environment. Similarly, if they intend to study history, the group will travel to the locations where the events occurred. There, lessons will be taught that encourage deep analysis of the events, often with the participation of local residents who recount the events exactly as they happened, without biases or interpretations. This valuable firsthand knowledge serves as input for profound learning.

—What an astonishing model! I can see that the system requires immense logistics, along with substantial resources and a tremendous linguistic ability on the part of the teacher.

—Well, I must tell you it's quite the opposite. Regarding the overall education costs, including, of course, the travel expenses to any part of the world for all the students and their tutor throughout the process, these are covered by the global education ministry's budget, so people don't have to invest resources in their children's education. Similarly, in every place the group visits, there is a standardized school residence, ensuring that the students always feel at home. Moreover, wherever the student groups go, they are warmly welcomed by the local community, who provide them with food and clothing during their stay, as in our society, we consider all children and youth as if they were our own. As for the logistics of the trips, they are very straightforward because nothing is improvised. Each year, teachers, supported by our advanced technology, plan the entire school year, so they know where they will travel and therefore which houses will be available for occupation. Regarding the communication aspect you mentioned, I must inform you that many centuries ago, the world adopted "Esperanto" as the official language. The entire planet speaks the same language, and although anyone is free to learn another language if they wish, they are aware that all information transfer is conducted through the official language.

—But you and I are speaking in my language. How is that possible?

—Although I have some knowledge of your language, the reason we can have such smooth communication is thanks to technology. A small electronic device implanted in my brain and controlled through this bracelet allows me to fluently speak any language, among many other functions. However, the decision for an individual to implant the chip or not is entirely personal, as in this society, freedom of choice is our most cherished value.

—Could you please tell me more about that technology you've mentioned?

—Of course, I will do that, but first, I would like to conclude with the topic of education. When a person reaches the age of twenty-two, it is considered that they have completed their phase of comprehensive education and, therefore, they are ready to choose whether they want to specialize in a profession or engage in an activity that they feel more identified with. By expressing their fullest potential, they will fulfill their life's purpose.

—Allow me a moment, please. Are you telling me that in this era, everyone pursues what they enjoy doing the most? Then, what happens to the jobs that nobody wants to do?

—I understand that it may be difficult for you to comprehend, so in order to clarify this point further, let me explain that we have advanced our technology to unprecedented levels compared to your time, and at the same time, we have kept it under our control and fully at the service of humanity.

That's how all the activities, jobs, and professions necessary for the smooth functioning of society, from the smallest tasks to global governance, are susceptible to being performed by artificial intelligence. In other words, we have designed a precise planetary system that can operate autonomously, although always under our continuous observation. However, individuals have the right, if they choose to do so, to replace machines in any area and perform the work themselves. In this regard, individuals are familiar with the minimum standards that must be met for the execution of any profession. Therefore, any innovation, style, or improvement proposed by a person when carrying out any activity not only gives them the satisfaction of doing a good job but also earns them well-deserved recognition from the entire community. We highly value human talent and always prefer it over activities performed by machines.

—What would happen if someone decides they don't want to work?

—In our society, the main priority is to ensure that every individual has the utmost freedom to choose their own path. So, if someone were to decide that they don't want to work, they would still receive the minimum resources necessary to live a dignified life. But why would someone prefer to remain idle instead of engaging in an activity they are truly passionate about, to the point where they would be willing to do it without any compensation?

—What you mention makes a lot of sense. Now the question that arises is, how do you manage to ensure that all people can receive the same benefit that guarantees them a good survival? That is why I made the comparison with the communist system.

—Yes, I understand your point. A long time ago, we realized that there have always been enough resources on the planet to meet the basic needs of the entire population. The real issue in your time is that you are not truly facing scarcity problems but rather issues of inequitable distribution of goods and resources. That's why, when we understood that the economy should operate autonomously and independently from politics and governmental systems, we were able to solve most of our problems.

Currently, we have a highly efficient global economic system that is designed to distribute goods and wealth among different regions of the planet and its inhabitants in a fair and equitable manner.

—Could you give me more details about how this efficient system works? I would also like to know, what do the leaders of different nations say about not having control over their own economies?

—In order for you to understand how our advanced economic system works, it is necessary to know that in the current model of global governance, we have eliminated the concept of countries and only have four geographic regions. If we were to reference them to your time, they would be constituted as follows:

The Northwest region, comprising Mexico, the United States, Canada, and Greenland.

The Southwest region, spanning from Guatemala to Argentina.

The Northeast region, encompassing the rest of Europe and Russia.

And finally, the largest region, the Southeast, which includes the entire African continent, as well as Oceania and the rest of Asia.

In this way, each region self-sustains and contributes the surplus of its goods and natural resources based on the needs of its peers. Similarly, each region receives what it requires without imposing further limits, relying on a high degree of common sense among the members of each zone.

Furthermore, all financial transactions are electronic, so physical money no longer exists. Individuals, who attend the "Place of Joy," as we call work, receive a salary based on their hours of service and the type of work they perform. The enormous accounting associated with this is carried out by an advanced artificial intelligence system that is dedicated to serving the planetary society.

—I'm very surprised to learn that countries and political leaders no longer exist! On the other hand, does that mean there are no big entrepreneurs or corporations? In that case, what is the incentive to specialize in something or start a business? —Mell asked, quite confused.

—In the present, the incentive to pursue any personal project is simply the fact that someone desires and decides to do so. We have achieved such an advanced organization that we truly ensure that everyone has equal opportunities to materialize their dreams, as long as it does not negatively affect the community in any way. So, if someone wishes to experience the journey of becoming a successful entrepreneur, they have the freedom to do so and, in the process, they could invite others to join their project or leverage available technology to achieve their goals.

On the other hand, the advanced financial system we designed is based on an innovative concept of complete transparency. This means that all electronic money circulating in the global economy could be perfectly traceable by anyone who chooses to do so. In this regard, the salary of each individual, the accumulated wealth of a company or individual, the profit margins added to any product or service, the legal contributions made by an organization or citizen, and even the financial resources of each region on the planet, are public data that can be accessed at any given moment by anyone. It was precisely thanks to this open financial structure that we were able to eliminate many of the conflicts that in the distant past led to wars.

—That means in this society there are no rich and poor individuals. Additionally, what is the incentive for personal growth if there is no competition, as it seems?

—Here, poverty doesn't exist. The government ensures that every individual born has everything they need to live until they reach their productive age and decide what they want to dedicate themselves to. However, there are individuals with a considerable accumulation of wealth, and this is because they chose to pursue that path and, through self-improvement, have achieved outstanding financial results. But unlike the time you come from, for this individual to reach that goal, they didn't have to take advantage of others or harm the environment. Furthermore, their comfortable economic condition doesn't generate criticism or envy from others, as everyone knows they could achieve the same outcome if they so choose.

As for the point you mentioned regarding competition, it occurs mainly in an autonomous sense. Our constant motivation is to surpass ourselves, striving to improve every day with the firm purpose of becoming the best version of ourselves. In this way, we always appreciate the work and effort of others, without feeling superior or threatened by them. We simply understand that we are all different, and each person decides their own destiny based on their own tastes and preferences.

—So in your culture, do competitive sports not exist either?

—That's an interesting point, thank you for bringing it up. Yes, sports do exist in our culture, and they are a significant part of our lifestyle because they help us stay healthy and constantly face new challenges. In this regard, individual sports such as athletics, swimming, and cycling are quite popular. However, there are also team sports, but with a notable difference in terms of the objective they pursue.

—In that case, could you please let me know if soccer is still played? As you can understand, I am English and, therefore, a huge fan of that sport.

—I understand your passion well, my good friend, and I believe this is the perfect example to address the topic that has arisen. Soccer is the most widely practiced team sport on the planet, and this is mainly because, quite often, the eleven players on each team are made up of individuals who have studied together for years. Here is where the first major difference arises: several teams are composed of both men and women. Another variation is that each team only has the eleven players who will participate in the matches, meaning there are no substitute players.

—What happens if someone gets injured or feels too tired to continue?

—In this sport, like any other, the most important thing is for all team members to have the maximum fun. Therefore, we believe that someone who doesn't participate in the game wouldn't be experiencing the highest enjoyment. However, anyone is free to leave the field if they decide to do so, and in this case, the rest of the team would continue playing without any issues. They would continue enjoying themselves regardless of being in a numerical disadvantage.

Regarding injuries, I must tell you that due to the new approach to the game, they are so rare that we could practically say they don't happen anymore. The main focus in the present soccer we play is not to try to score the most goals, but to attempt the most spectacular plays while aiming to score a goal. The opposing team will do their best to obstruct their opponent and take the ball away, then demonstrate their skills while also attempting to score. All of this happens without displays of violence and in an atmosphere of fraternity.

So, when each player or team performs a fabulous play, whether it ends in a goal or not, everyone on the field celebrates as if they belong to the same team. This allows the spectators to enjoy each match to the fullest. In this way, all team sports are practiced as if they were entertaining sports circus performances.

—You could say that teams are like a sort of Harlem Globetrotters in every sport!

—I couldn't have described it better, my respected gentleman.

—What motivated you to make these peculiar changes?

—Very simple, it was the feeling of unity. We realized that we couldn't feel truly good if another being experienced any affliction because of us. In this sense, we stopped promoting the societal model where someone had to lose for there to be a winner, and where people were primarily educated through a system of rewards and punishments.

That's why, by embracing this elevated expression of unity at all levels and eliminating the concept of countries, we found that there were no borders to defend and therefore no armies to maintain. In fact, it's interesting to mention that before reaching our present state and during the arduous process filled with long days of work and negotiations that led to the progressive reduction of military spending, we were surprised by the rapid financial surplus we achieved solely through the implementation of that measure. And let me tell you that were one of the reasons that gave us confidence that we were on the right path.

—Then, who governs and under what model of political organization?

—Well, the government model we have is similar to what you know as a federal system, although with notable differences. In our case, there is no figure of a president, prime minister, or king. Instead, we have four "Representative Leaders," one for each region, who, along with their respective teams, are responsible for reaching agreements and communicating decisions that affect the entire global community. Likewise, each region is divided into sectors that have a similar organizational structure, and this continues until reaching the most basic unit called a "Clan," which is primarily composed of the eleven individuals who received their education together and often includes their closest relatives.

—I heard you say that there are four individuals who make the decisions. What would happen if they can't reach an agreement or if a vote ends in a tie? How would they resolve the matter? I also have another question. You mentioned earlier that everyone has the freedom to pursue any project as long as it doesn't harm others. I would like to know, who determines if an idea could be unfavorable or not? And how would the person react if they are prevented from pursuing it?

—Those are very interesting questions, my dear Thomas, but before answering them, may I offer you something to drink? Tell me, would you prefer coffee or tea?

—I prefer coffee, with a little sugar. And I would like to take this opportunity to thank you for the gesture —the historian expressed courteously.

At that moment, the lady went to a corner of the modern office where a simple yet beautiful kitchen space was located. She took the coffee from a small manual grinder in the corner and retrieved a moka pot from a cabinet. Instantly, she began preparing the beverage.

—Is that what I think it is? Are you using a stovetop espresso maker to brew coffee? —Mell exclaimed with incredulous amazement.

—That's right, professor. I enjoy making coffee in the traditional way of the 20th century.

—I thought with all this technology, perhaps the cup of coffee would materialize in the air or a robot would come out from a compartment in the wall and serve it to us!

—Hahaha! Imagine you would say that. Well, let me tell you that, although it may sound contradictory, technology, when used wisely, has made us more human. I say this because, after deep reflections on many aspects of our existence, we have decided to return to ancient customs in various aspects of our lives —the lady responded, handing the gentleman an aromatic coffee she had added a natural sweetener to.

—How is it possible that things are like this?

—Well, let me explain. As absurd as it may sound, you must understand that the way I prepared this coffee is closely related to how we make decisions in the present. For a long time now, one of the main applications of our advanced technology is the execution of complex simulations. Through these simulations, we can predict with great precision the most likely outcome of any idea or decision we intend to pursue. These simulations rely on a vast database that accurately describes human behavior, as well as that of other living beings and even the planet itself. The insights gained from these simulations provide us with the perfect framework for making the best decisions. In this regard, if a situation arises where, during the analysis of an issue by the representative leaders, they have divided opinions; the decision that generates the best impact for the greatest number of people will always prevail. And we are confident that all those involved will feel satisfied by adopting the most beneficial resolution.

In this regard, I can tell you that when it comes to food, we have returned to practices that are ancestral to us, particularly in terms of cultivation, care, and harvesting methods. Currently, in our crops, we only use organic fertilizers, and we dedicate special care to soil maintenance and rotation. Similarly, we apply these healthy habits to the natural way in which we prepare and cook our food. In fact, many products that were popular in your time no longer exist today because our food is free from harmful chemical components.

—But many products in my time had chemicals to preserve them, and they only cause harm if consumed in excess.

—Not all the chemicals you use have that purpose. Regarding consumption, you raise valid points about the discourse used by marketing campaigns of large corporations in your time to prioritize economic benefits over collective health. It is worth questioning what is meant by "excessive consumption." Is it a matter of time, quantity, or both? Who defines and tabulates these data? Are these determinations made by the same companies that commercialize the products?

In our approach, when we prioritize health above all else, we utilize technology to enhance the organic processes of agricultural production from the past. If a simulation study indicates any potential risks to people, the product, project, or decision in question is discarded. The individuals or leaders who proposed the idea will be the first to abandon it, as they always act in the best interest of the collective well-being. The goal is to ensure that every decision and action we take is beneficial to the entire community.

—I imagine that you lead a very healthy life. How is the health situation these days?

—You are absolutely right, we lead a healthy existence in all aspects of our being, and as a result, the longevity of the population has increased significantly. For instance, how old do you think I am?

—Judging by your appearance, I would venture to say that we are contemporaries, so I estimate you must be around 65-years-old.

—Hahaha! Allow me to thank you for the compliment, Professor. Well, I am actually 128-years-old, and currently our life expectancy is around one hundred and eighty years, so I still have a few springs left to live.

—You have left me speechless! But tell me, how did you achieve such an astonishing feat?

—In a simple way. Health ceased to be a business and became a paramount and entirely public matter. At the same time, we focused our greatest efforts on preventive care. We are all aware of the best way to treat our perfect mechanism called the body. Therefore, our diet is very healthy, but we go beyond that. Our thoughts and spirituality are also elevated, so the combination of all these elements allows us to live many years. In the field of medicine, the focus is primarily on research. The advancements made in the use of stem cells have been impressive and highly beneficial. While surgeries are occasionally performed, the science developed around picotechnology, which is a thousand times smaller than nanotechnology, provides extraordinary results with minimally invasive techniques.

In addition to all of this, we have learned to coexist in true harmony with the planet, and therefore, any decision we make always prioritizes human beings and Mother Earth above all else. As a result, environmental pollution has practically become a legend from your era.

—Now that you mention that point, I would like to know, what is your main source of energy?

—In the present, our main source of energy comes from freshwater. We have developed highly efficient systems that use this vital liquid as fuel, and the by-product is still water. This innovative technology was developed centuries after the last war by scientists who worked in one of the few areas that experienced less radiation effects and also have abundant water resources. I am referring to the vast Amazonia. That is why, in recognition of the work of those pioneering technologists, the center of the global government was established right in the heart of this jungle, where we are currently located.

—I must confess that when I emerged from the tunnel, I felt very confused because I never imagined that in the future, nature and modern constructions would blend together so perfectly.

—I understand perfectly, Mr. Thomas. That is the most common reaction from everyone who visits us. Well, we must conclude this entertaining conversation as the portal will soon close, so it's time for you to return home. Please let me know briefly if there's anything else you would like to know.

—I can tell you that my mind is filled with over a thousand questions, but given the haste, I just want to know, why out of so many human beings, was I chosen for this encounter?

—Your concern is very relevant, professor. I must tell you that you are not, have not been, nor will you be the only person to visit us, and as for why you are one of the chosen ones, the answer is simple: our mission is to contact influential people from your time who have the ability to carry our message, in order to try to change the course of history and consequently prevent the worst war humanity has ever experienced and its effects.

—But you have already mentioned that the war happened and that it even served as the catalyst for you to reach the level of consciousness you exhibit now. So, if you alter the course of history, wouldn't you also be changing your present? —asked the perplexed gentleman.

—If you understood the concept of non-linearity of time, you might grasp that our society represents a potentially probable future that humanity can reach through less painful paths. It is true that the nuclear conflict served as a catalyst to reach the present we live in, but in balance, the lives lost, the irreparable damage to many places, the severe impact on the planet, and the genetic mutations suffered by many survivors do not in any way justify the path taken to achieve technological advancement and the level of consciousness we currently have.

—In this case, what do you suggest I do? How can I contribute?

—I greatly appreciate your willingness. The best way in which we believe time travelers from your era can help redirect the course of history is by transmitting as much information as possible about the real possibility for humanity, especially its leaders, to change the practices that tend to generate conflicts, as well as the actions they employ to try to solve them. The suggested communication strategy is important to reach as many people as possible, but particularly it should be directed towards the younger generations. By encouraging critical and independent thinking, they can avoid being entirely absorbed by the valueless system that prevails in the 21st century.

—All that you mention is very good. But how should I carry out this mission? What exactly should I transmit? What tools will I have at my disposal?

—Being a renowned historian and academic, we know that your opinion is highly valued by the society of your time. It is for this reason, along with your immense human sensitivity, that we chose you to embark on this unique journey. However, it is important to note that you will not be alone in such an ambitious task. There is a significant group of individuals, as influential as yourself, who have also visited us, and we are confident that by working together, you can create the conditions to bring about the desired change.

As for the message we want to be transmitted, it mainly revolves around inviting the human race to react and start working together towards increasingly higher goals, thus ensuring that they will reach our level of consciousness in the future. To achieve this, we suggest that you place special emphasis on the following aspects:

All of you are co-creators of your experiences, both individually and collectively, so it is time for you to take responsibility for your actions and become truly aware of your mistakes in order to correct them and prevent their repetition. By focusing on enhancing your virtues and successes, you can shape a brighter future.

Understanding that the ultimate truth is that all of you are spiritual beings having a human experience. Therefore, any conflict that arises will always have a spiritual underpinning, and only by working on that level can you achieve true solutions. This is why real and lasting peace in the world can only be possible when each individual will experience genuine inner peace.

Embracing the urgency to embark without delay on the path that many beings have pointed out and many others continue to show. You must stop perceiving yourselves as separate from one another and from the Creator, for everything in the universe is intrinsically interconnected. By experiencing yourselves as united, as one human family, you must courageously take the necessary decisions to ensure the achievement of goals that provide the greatest benefit for all. And if, as expected, doubts and hesitations arise during this challenging and extensive journey, remember that you can always ask yourselves: How would love act in this circumstance?

Likewise, you must internalize that true change will only occur when, together, you are capable of envisioning the grandest version that you can reach as a human race. At that moment, you must embrace the values that uphold that vision and transform them into the foundations of your new culture. In this regard, a profound educational transformation will be essential, incorporating valuable concepts such as responsibility, honesty, respect, and transparency into the formation of the new individual. Teach people that the best way to practice justice is by acting in a way that doesn't require correction. And that truth, like natural laws, provides the best framework for living healthily and harmoniously. If a law isn't easily understood and justified, then it should be thoroughly examined. If it needs explanation because it's not perceived clearly and evidently, it may primarily serve the interests of the group proposing it.

So, and finally, I assure you that from now on, we will stay in communication to support you in the arduous mission of awakening humanity from its slumber. So, don't be surprised if you suddenly start receiving valuable information through different unexpected channels that will aid in this monumental task.

—I am immensely grateful for the honor of being chosen to be part of this prestigious group of individuals. I want to express that I will dedicate myself with utmost effort to transmit the profound message I have received —said the historian, visibly moved.

—Thank you, professor. I expected nothing less from a man with such extraordinary qualities as yours. Now, allow me to accompany you to the square so you can return home —replied the pleasant lady as she guided him back to the portal.

During the journey towards the tunnel, they both discussed a topic that piqued the academic's particular interest: the system of laws and the administration of justice in that advanced society. The hostess explained that they had very few laws, thanks to the sense of unity they expressed and the practice of coherent and shared common sense, which made the application of numerous rules unnecessary. As for the way justice was served, she indicated that if someone committed an act that could be considered a wrongdoing towards another individual, society, or the planet, the first step would be to evaluate the mental state of that person. If the diagnosis revealed any kind of imbalance, appropriate medical treatment would be sought. On the other hand, if it was determined that the offender was of sound mind, the information regarding the incident, including the arguments of the involved parties, would be compiled and presented to the global community through an advanced consultation mechanism. For one week, the entire population could learn about the incident and voice their opinions. If the person was found responsible, the corrective action would be chosen based on a limited list of options, usually derived from similar cases. Once a decision was reached by consensus, the members of the individual's clan would ensure the enforcement of the restorative action. Regarding this point, the lady explained that on the rare occasions when such incidents occurred, the usual measures included extra service hours to help compensate for the damage caused or, in other cases, temporary isolation to allow the person to deeply reflect on what had transpired. At that moment in the conversation, the traveler was astonished to discover how radically different the judicial system was in the future society, where all inhabitants of the planet took turns acting as global jurors or judges.

Once the professor returned to his everyday life, he felt particularly impacted as he noticed how Dinna's promise was fulfilled to the fullest. As soon as he started presenting the immense capacity that human beings have to evolve towards a higher level of consciousness in all the spaces he participated in, he found himself surrounded by a tremendous number of people who joined him in his message. At the same time, he received a substantial amount of related information from all directions.

From that moment on, that sort of contemporary army of Don Quixotes embarked on the ambitious crusade to try to change the world in order to achieve a better future for all of humanity. They knew that the mission would not be short or easy, but the satisfaction of inspiring through such a noble and valuable ideal gave them the necessary momentum to continue despite the adversities. So, it didn't take long for them to feel pleasantly surprised, as they understood —as had happened to so many others before them—, that in their eagerness to improve the world, they inevitably ended up transforming into better beings, and their lives became obligatory references for the new generations who chose to follow the extraordinary paths laid out by them."

LIFE MISSION

After receiving well-deserved popularity for the publication of his highly original essay, Glem continued his university career and successfully completed it in an exceptional manner.

On the day of his graduation, as Glem made his way towards the stage, the master of ceremonies announced that he had been the only student to receive the summa cum laude distinction in his graduating class. At that moment, everyone in the crowded auditorium stood up, giving a thunderous ovation to the accomplished young man. As he stood before the university authorities, including his beloved aunt Lena, who was waiting to present him with his diploma, Glem was taken aback when a brief pause occurred in the formal protocol, allowing another distinguished figure to join them on the podium. It was none other than Mr.

Arthur Smith, slowly approaching with a beautiful medal in hand. Once he stood by his daughter's side, they both presented the honors to Glem, accompanied by heartfelt hugs, which Glem reciprocated with overwhelming emotion.

Immediately after, the celebration began as Glem's family and friends gathered at the cozy restaurant "La Roma," the chosen venue for the festivities. The atmosphere was filled with merriment when suddenly, the graduate called for everyone's attention.

—I want to thank all of you for being here with me. It means a lot to have your presence on this special day —Glem spoke, visibly excited—. But most importantly, I want to acknowledge the three most important women in my life. My mother, who with her infinite love has always been my guide throughout my twenty-five years, I feel that my greatest blessing has been to be born from her womb. My aunt Lena, who has unconditionally supported me in the development of many of my projects, which have helped shape me into the person I am today. And my beloved Sandra, who was my inseparable companion for so long, and now, is the being who inspires the most sublime acts of a beautiful and conscious love that I never imagined I could feel. But there is another aspect I would like to mention. Many consider me a brilliant person, but let me tell you something; Sandra Rizzi is probably the smartest woman you will ever meet in your lives. To support my argument, I'll just say that when she agreed to be my girlfriend, she immediately decided to study psychology. Clearly, she did this with the intention of acquiring the tools and knowledge necessary to stay by the side of a madman like me.

At that moment, everyone burst into loud laughter. Blushing, Sandra watched as several people approached her, congratulating her. And amidst the commotion, the young man made a signal, and suddenly, exquisite instrumental music filled the air, causing everyone to stop talking and focus on the beautiful performance. Glem had found the charming trio of Italian musicians again, and as they played Andrea Bocelli's beautiful song "Con te partirò" (Time to Say Goodbye), they approached where the young man stood. Once they positioned themselves behind him, he took out a box from his pocket and, kneeling down, he asked his girlfriend:

—My love, will you continue to accompany me on the wonderful journey of discovering who we are and what our mission in life is?" —Glem said, as he presented a beautiful engagement ring to her.

—Yes, I accept! I only wish to walk that path with you —Sandra exclaimed, jumping with excitement—. Besides, you know that I need you, as you'll be the best case study for my psychology postgraduate program —she added, laughing. With the ring now on her finger, she invited her boyfriend to stand up and immediately planted a passionate kiss on his lips.

All the people in the place were celebrating that wonderful event and congratulating the beautiful couple. In this way, the evening concluded with a great spirit of joy.

After those moments, Glem faced the decision of what to do with his career. In this regard, he received a variety of job offers, including some government proposals as well as opportunities in academia. However, to the surprise of those who were expecting him to join their organizations, the brilliant young man turned down all the received propositions. He wanted to find a way to make a difference in society but from a different environment. Additionally, a year earlier, his fiancée had started a successful career in the corporate world, and her organization requested her to relocate to the city of Toronto. Faced with this situation, the couple decided to move to the big city, but before that, they agreed to have a simple yet beautiful wedding. The ceremony took place in the same house where, twenty years ago, their parents had gotten married. This time, there were no notable absences during the wonderful celebration, and the homeowner, Mr. Arthur Smith, acted as an extraordinary host. At the end of the emotional evening, Enzo Rizzi took the floor and addressed the happy couple, saying.

—I want to congratulate my little sister on her marriage. And I must confess that this great moment brings me as much joy as relief because now there is someone else who will have the responsibility of taking care of her. However, what I truly don't know is what I will do with so much free time —at that moment, laughter echoed throughout the hall—. I also want to congratulate Glem and welcome him to the family. I know that in the past we weren't the best of friends, but getting to know you better has made me admire you, and I hope that we can become like brothers —that's how Enzo concluded his heartfelt words, while his sister blew him kisses from a distance, and the groom nodded and sent him a signal of a hug.

As soon as the couple settled in Toronto, Glem knew he had to engage in some form of employment. After deep introspection, he acknowledged that his greatest passion was teaching. However, he wasn't entirely drawn to the university setting, as he felt somewhat at odds with certain principles that underpinned the conservative model of higher education.

This led him to inquire about the environment that best suited his ideal job, and it was at that moment that he made the decision to approach the Waldorf School in Toronto to offer himself as a teacher. He had been deeply impressed when a magnificent book fell into his hands, introducing him to the unique philosophy of these schools. It even served as inspiration for him to devise the advanced system of holistic education he presented in his futuristic narrative.

The fact is that the unique Waldorf educational model, born in Germany in the early 20th century and now present in many schools around the world, offers a holistic approach to education. It prioritizes the physical, emotional, artistic, intellectual, and spiritual development of students. The teacher plays a fundamental role in the teaching process, accompanying the students for several years, fostering a close relationship of trust and deep mutual understanding.

In this educational approach, learning is based on a participatory method that encourages individuals to have direct experiences in exploring their environment. During early education, the focus is on activities related to nature, art, and play, avoiding the use of textbooks and technology as much as possible. In primary and secondary education, there is a strong emphasis on developing analytical skills, logical reasoning, and critical thinking in relation to the subjects taught.

Regarding assessment methods, these schools offer an innovative approach. Instead of focusing on quantitative analysis, continuous observation of the student's cognitive, artistic, emotional, and social aspects is emphasized. The primary goal is to recognize the individual progress of each student in all these areas.

Once Glem made contact with the school, he was quickly called in for an interview. As expected, the school administration was delighted with his personality and profile. Fortunately, a vacancy had recently opened up as one of the teachers had decided to move with their family to another province in Canada, so Glen was able to get the position.

After completing a series of preparatory courses, which he excelled in, Glem was appointed as the lead teacher. At that moment, he was assigned a joyful group of children, aged six to seven, whom he would educate under that unique philosophy for the next eight years.

During his first year as a teacher, Glem often expressed that he couldn't imagine finding another job that would bring him greater satisfaction. His statement held true, as he no longer felt the need to embark on the fantastic time-traveling journeys that had once stirred his emotions. At that moment, he was fully immersed in the joy of freely sharing his pedagogical talent and artistic skills for the benefit of teaching and shaping those wonderful beings. He often remarked that he learned much more from his students than he could ever teach them. His originality in delivering classes and his deep ability to connect with his students quickly set him apart from his colleagues, earning him the genuine affection of both his group of students and their parents.

With only one year left to complete his students' education, and having demonstrated an extraordinary performance, the school's board called upon Glem to invite him to be part of an exciting project. The owners of the Waldorf School in Toronto had decided to open another branch in the city and expressed to the young man that, due to his age, high professional profile, and abundant innovative capacity, they wanted to transfer him to the new school. In addition to his teaching activities, he would also assume significant leadership responsibilities with sufficient autonomy. The young man, almost without hesitation, accepted the proposal, and immediately filled with uncontrollable excitement; he made his way home to share the news with his beloved wife.

—My love, I want to tell you some wonderful news! —Glem exclaimed, immensely excited.

—My love, I'm thrilled to see you so joyful. I also have something amazing to share with you, but please, tell me yours first —Sandra replied, impatient to hear the news that had put her husband in such a state.

—I was offered to be the leader of a new Waldorf school in the city, and in addition to continuing to teach, they will allow me to organize the institution in my own style. So I accepted because I feel that this is the best opportunity I have to try and shape future leaders who could make a positive impact on the world. Now please, tell me what you want to share with me. I also notice that you're quite excited.

—I'm so thrilled about what you're telling me, my love, and to add to the reasons for celebration, I want you to know that we're going to be parents. Today, I went to the doctor, and they confirmed that I'm one month pregnant —Sandra said, as they embraced each other tightly, feeling overjoyed in each other's arms.

—¡At this moment, I feel like the happiest man in the universe! And also the luckiest, to receive all these blessings together. I am infinitely grateful to life for all the manifestations I experience in my existence.

Time passed, and a beautiful baby girl, named Hannah, came into the world in a home filled with love. She was a baby with light brown hair, eyes the same emerald green as her mother's, slightly lighter cinnamon skin than her father's, and a radiant aura that foreshadowed she would be a great being of light.

When her grandmother Ada held her for the first time, she felt as if her heart was divided into two equal parts, because from that moment she knew she would love her with the same intensity as her son. Moreover, her joy was immense knowing that she would always be able to enjoy her presence, as a few months prior, Glem had asked her to join him in the project of the new school, and without hesitation, she accepted her son's request. So by that time, she had already moved to Toronto.

That beautiful little girl continued to grow, expressing herself freely within a harmonious and loving environment, far from excessive technology and immersed in a peaceful routine, devoid of the countless activities to which modern parents subject their children in order to discover their talents. And so, one day, a peculiar dialogue took place between Hannah and her father, which prompted deep reflection in Glem.

Father and daughter were in the attic, organizing some things that had been used in the recent celebration of the cheerful girl's sixth birthday. Suddenly, while her dad was distracted with his task, she, as if guided by an invisible force, walked slowly towards the back of the small room.

As she pulled a sheet covering an object that appeared tall and sturdy from her perspective, she revealed the homemade quantum machine. At that moment, she turned to her father and asked.

—Daddy! Will I ever be able to travel in your machine?

Glem's reaction was one of complete bewilderment. How could a girl who had been raised without exposure to fiction stories and technology think that the wooden contraption, resembling more of a pyramid-shaped piece of furniture, was a machine she could travel in? In that moment, Glem, delving into the vast knowledge he had accumulated through years of curious exploration, remembered that souls bring with them a wealth of information and experiences when they incarnate, often beyond rational explanation. However, despite his recent realization, he couldn't shake off his astonishment completely. So, approaching his daughter, he lovingly took her in his arms and said.

—Of course, my precious Hannah, when you grow up, I will teach you how to travel in my machine —in that moment, Glem had a premonition that the stories of time travel were far from over, and that they would undoubtedly continue for generations to come.

THE END

ABOUT THE AUTHOR

Carlos Laya is a Venezuelan, an Electronic Engineer, Master in Marketing, Broadcaster, and a passionate writer of short stories and novels. As an empirical historian he is the author of the radio program 'Universal Characters,' which airs on Stereo 97.9FM in Valencia, Venezuela. He has a variety of articles published in business profile magazines, in areas related to leadership, management, marketing, sales, and customer service. Based in Canada, married with two children, he enjoys traveling around the world, exploring new cultures, and treasuring unforgettable moments.

Contact:

 carloslaya.autor@gmail.com

@carloslaya.autor

carloslaya.autor

Manufactured by Amazon.ca
Acheson, AB

12416431R00140